new
facts of
life for
women

Also by the authors:

IN CASE OF EMERGENCY: *What to Do Until the Doctor Arrives*

new facts of life for women

by annette francis benjamin
and bry benjamin, m.d.

prentice-hall, inc.
englewood cliffs, new jersey

to all women . . . and especially those we love

New Facts of Life for Women
by Annette Francis Benjamin and Bry Benjamin, M.D.

© 1969 by Annette Francis Benjamin and Bry Benjamin, M.D.
All rights reserved. No part of this book may be
reproduced in any form or by any means, except for
the inclusion of brief quotations in a review, without
permission in writing from the publisher.
13–612564–6
Library of Congress Catalog Card Number: 69-13790
Printed in the United States of America • T
Prentice-Hall International, Inc., London
Prentice-Hall of Australia, Pty. Ltd., Sydney
Prentice-Hall of Canada, Ltd., Toronto
Prentice-Hall of India Private Ltd., New Delhi
Prentice-Hall of Japan, Inc., Tokyo

Acknowledgments

We are grateful to Stewart L. Marcus, M.D., Associate Professor of Obstetrics and Gynecology, Cornell University Medical College, New York City, for reading the manuscript and contributing constructive comments, and to the following professors who aided us in areas of their special competence: Myron I. Buchman, M.D., Clinical Associate Professor of Obstetrics and Gynecology, Cornell University Medical College; Herbert Conway, M.D., Clinical Professor of Surgery, Cornell University Medical College; John MacLeod, Ph.D., Associate Professor of Anatomy, Cornell University Medical College; S. Frank Redo, M.D., Clinical Associate Professor of Surgery, Cornell University Medical College; and Norman Simon, M.D., Associate Professor of Radiotherapy, Mount Sinai School of Medicine, New York City.

In addition, we owe gratitude to Dr. Julius Mark, Rabbi Emeritus, Congregation Emanu-El of the City of New York

(Temple Emanu-El), and Rev. William H. Genné, Coordinator of the Commission on Marriage and Family, National Council of the Churches of Christ in the United States of America, for reading "The Jewish Viewpoint" and "The Protestant Viewpoint," respectively, in the chapter entitled "Historical Viewpoints on Abortion."

We are especially indebted to Miss Doris Lowe, Head Reference Librarian, Cornell University Medical College, for her indefatigable efforts and invaluable assistance in locating source material and for encouraging us in our objectives.

Foreword

The twentieth century is witnessing unprecedented achievements in all the sciences, many of which are responsible for rapidly changing attitudes toward sex in the very largest sense. There are new outlooks on varieties of human behavior, on family planning, on legal and social solutions to problems that women and men have long faced in silence. It may soon come to pass that nowhere in the world will a woman be unaware of her individual sense of biologic responsibility—in contrast to being, until recently, the passive biological receptacle and nourisher of the seed of mankind.

Today's woman suffers from two kinds of communication distortion: the persistent relics of taboos and secrecy leading to lack of knowledge and, on the other hand, a daily barrage of premature, often conflicting and sensational, bulletins of incomplete information. Very much as medical care is being increasingly considered a human right in societies which can afford it, so the proper knowledge of one's biological role and potentiality and the means of fulfilling these will be considered the right of everyone.

It is the purpose of this book to present to women a clear and accurate picture of what is happening in the world of science that can benefit them in their own personal worlds.

THE AUTHORS

Contents

Acknowledgments vii

Foreword ix

PART I—BIRTH CONTROL

Chapter	1	The History of Birth Control	3
Chapter	2	The "Best" Birth Control Method	11
Chapter	3	Oral Contraceptives	15
Chapter	4	Intrauterine Devices	23
Chapter	5	Other Effective Birth Control Methods	27

Chapter	6	Less Effective Birth Control Methods	35
Chapter	7	Sterilization	41
Chapter	8	Contraception for Minors	47
Chapter	9	Contraception in the Future	51

PART II—THE ABORTION REVOLUTION

Chapter	10	Historical Viewpoints on Abortion	55
Chapter	11	Abortion Laws in Foreign Countries	65
Chapter	12	Abortion Laws in the United States	73
Chapter	13	Therapeutic Abortion	79

PART III—THE PREGNANT WOMAN

Chapter	14	Tests for Pregnancy	87
Chapter	15	Safer Pregnancy	91
Chapter	16	Control of Labor	99
Chapter	17	Sexual Relations During and After Pregnancy	105

PART IV—THE UNBORN CHILD

Chapter	18	The Rh Factor	111
Chapter	19	Birth Defects	121

PART V—THE NEWBORN CHILD

| Chapter 20 | The Transition from Fetus to Newborn | 145 |
| Chapter 21 | The Problem of Mental Retardation | 155 |

PART VI—THE INFERTILE COUPLE

Chapter 22	Sterility and Fertility	165
Chapter 23	Diagnosis and Treatment of Male Infertility	173
Chapter 24	Diagnosis and Treatment of Female Infertility	179

PART VII—THE OLDER WOMAN

Chapter 25	The Menopause	197
Chapter 26	Diagnosis and Treatment of Breast Cancer	201
Chapter 27	Cosmetic Surgery	207
Chapter 28	Sex in the Later Years	215

Bibliography 219

Index 231

PART 1

BIRTH CONTROL

1

The History of Birth Control

The belief that storks brought babies began with the ancient Teutons. The bewilderment engendered by this idea could not possibly have equaled the astonishment of the first people to realize that sexual intercourse "brought" babies.

This awesome revelation probably came late in man's intellectual development. The reason for this, according to social anthropologist E. S. Hartland, is that primitive man's only measure of time was the period from sunrise to sunrise. He had no calendars, no clocks, no comprehension of why the seasons came and went.

In early societies girls as young as six and seven years of age were used for sexual relations, and then, as now, pregnancies did not result. Many primitive peoples considered the state of menstruation a result of internal injury or sickness—the "normal" healthy woman being either too young or too old (or ceaselessly pregnant or lactating) to produce a menstrual flow. Infertility in both sexes must have prevented many pregnancies; and miscarriages, probably in even greater incidence than today—but unrecognized—must have further increased man's perplexity about the causes of pregnancy.

One can speculate that man's growing economic dependence upon animals may have instructed him in animal husbandry, with obvious lessons in reproduction to be translated to his own kind. Once the dawn of realization came to man that a baby was the direct end result of the sexual act of several months before, his attempts to control birth, and therefore, conception, became a never-ending challenge to his ingenuity. People in almost every culture have endeavored to control the size of their families, many cultures having resorted to abortion and infanticide, most cultures having experimented with various combinations of roots and herbs to prevent conception. An amazing number of mechanical and medicinal methods of controlling fertility were developed through the centuries. Most were probably ineffective.

The ideas embodied in all current birth control methods are as old as the Bible, ancient Egypt, and ancient Rome: medicines to be taken by the male or female, mechanical devices to be worn by the male or inserted into the female, and variations of the timing and positioning of intercourse.

The medical Ebers Papyrus (about 1550 B.C.) contains perhaps the first written reference to a contraceptive tampon. Made of lint and soaked with acacia and honey, it was to be inserted into the vagina before intercourse. Acacia, during fermentation, breaks down into lactic acid, one of the active spermatocidal agents used in contraceptive jellies today.

Other substances used for vaginal suppositories included eagle excrement and the dung of camels, crocodiles, and elephants. Elephant dung has a degree of acidity that could well have made it an effective contraceptive agent!

Among the multitudes of other birth control agents and methods used through the ages were: cabbage blossoms, camphor, cedar oil, seaweed, gunpowder tea, lemon-juice douche (possibly partially effective), olive oil, parsley, pomegranate, alum, hoof parings of a mule, and foam from a camel's mouth.

Holding one's breath, stepping over a grave, or wearing an amulet on the left thigh were also considered to be effective. (As late as 1888 the best advice some doctors could give, as recorded in the medical literature, was: "Before going to bed, drink a glass of cold water and don't touch another thing all night.")

Condoms made from sheep's bladders were used by the sophisticated men of Imperial Rome. This type of contraceptive, however, did not become well known until Fallopius in 1564 wrote of its application in the prevention of the spread of syphilis. In 1671 it is recorded that Madame de Sévigné wrote her daughter Françoise Marguerite a letter in which she condemned the condom as "armor against enjoyment and a spider web against danger."

In Casanova's *Mémoires* the famous lover makes reference to his use of condoms for contraception and prevention of venereal disease. He was anything but enthusiastic about them when he wrote: "I do not care to shut myself up in a piece of dead skin in order to prove that I am perfectly alive."

Boswell, in his *London Journal,* November 25, 1782, referred to being able to enjoy a woman "in Armour," because of its apparent success in preventing venereal infection. Condoms were in popular use in eighteenth-century brothels. By the middle of the nineteenth century mass production of condoms had been made possible by the vulcanization of rubber. It is estimated that in the United States the current annual production of condoms is between 700 and 800 million.

In a lecture presented by Dr. Alan F. Guttmacher* before the fifty-first annual Assembly of the Interstate Postgraduate Medical Association at Washington, D.C., in 1966, the world-renowned obstetrician-gynecologist speculated on the origins of the intrauterine device. "Camel herders invented the intrauterine device (IUD), perhaps a thousand years ago. A pregnant camel's disposition is rather unpleasant, and she prefers to kneel rather than walk. It was discovered that

---

* President of Planned Parenthood—World Population.

putting a stone in each cornu (horn) of the camel's uterus would prevent pregnancy."

Birth control first became a public matter in the nineteenth century after economist Malthus foresaw the horrors of overpopulation in his famous essay of 1798. The powerful English labor leader and social reformer Francis Place, who founded the birth control movement, was aware of Malthus' ideas, and in the 1820's distributed handbills recommending coitus interruptus and the vaginal sponge. He was the first to be concerned with limiting the size of families to prevent poverty and raise living standards.

The birth control movement in the United States was started in the 1830's by Dr. Charles Knowlton and social theorist Robert Dale Owen. Knowlton's contribution to the long history of birth control was support of postcoital douching, which he felt was a good method because it was harmless, cheap, and involved no interruption or discomfort during intercourse; it also fitted in with his philosophy that control of conception was the woman's responsibility. Knowlton served a three-month prison sentence for the publication of his pamphlet *The Fruits of Philosophy*, which gave enormous publicity to birth control methods.

In the 1870's two trials in England brought more public attention to the subject. Mrs. Annie Besant and Charles Bradlaugh, organizers of the Freethought Publishing Company whose purpose was to print and sell Knowlton's work, were tried in 1877 but found not guilty. Another publisher of birth control information, Edward Truelove, did not fare as well. He was found guilty and sentenced to a four-month prison term.

By the second half of the nineteenth century, birth control found an increasing number of supporters. In the United States Dr. D. Soule published his highly progressive view that conception control should be used for the spacing of children, especially by couples whose marriages were not harmonious.

The cervical cap and the vaginal diaphragm, two inventions of this period, were mentioned along with douches, tampons, withdrawal, and the safe period, in *The Wife's Handbook* by Dr. H.A. Allbutt of Scotland. His reward for his efforts was the removal of his name from the medical register by the Royal College of Physicians of Edinburgh, with the accusation that he "published and exposed for sale an indecent publication."

In nineteenth-century America more advocates and opponents of contraception were expounding their views. In 1848 John Humphrey Noyes, a licensed Congregational minister who was educated at Yale Theological School, founded a community near Oneida, New York. In this experiment in communal living great emphasis was placed upon the full satisfaction of the female. Noyes introduced a method of birth control in which there is normal intercourse without ejaculation, referred to as male continence, Karezza, or coitus reservatus. (The Oneida community actually began in Putney, Vermont, but orthodox church leaders forced the community to leave, as they strongly objected to the community's belief in and practice of Complex Marriage, in which everyone in the community was considered married to everyone else.)

A father and son medical team by the name of Foote further advanced the reasons for contraception. The elder physician felt that birth control was desirable in cases of poverty, ill health, predisposition to mental illness, and physical deformity. The younger Foote suggested its use to decrease infant mortality by reducing the number of births.

In 1873 Congress passed a law making it a criminal offense to distribute birth control information through the mail. This law, instigated by Anthony Comstock, head of The Society for the Suppression of Vice, covered obscene literature and articles of immoral use—the latter category including articles pertaining to methods of contraception and abortion. In 1890 Dr. John Reynolds, at that time president of The American Gynecological Society, opposed birth control and sex education as well, expressing his strong viewpoint that sex education led to low moral standards.

The advent of the twentieth century brought Mrs. Margaret Sanger, the most famous nurse since Florence Nightingale, into the forefront as the central figure in the organization of the birth control movement in the United States. The revolutionary idea that no woman should ever bear a child she does not want was instilled in Mrs. Sanger during the period of her life when she nursed the poor of New York City's lower East Side, where she observed that mothers who desperately needed birth control advice were not receiving it from doctors. It is thought that the term "birth control" was first used by her in *The Woman Rebel* (April 1914), a magazine that attacked the restrictive legislation of the Comstock Law. Mrs. Sanger founded in 1917 The American Birth Control League which in 1942 changed its name to The Planned Parenthood Federation of America. It was not until 1923 that she opened the first birth control clinic in the United States.

The Comstock Law of 1873 was tested in 1936 by Dr. Hannah Stone, who imported vaginal diaphragms from Japan, which were subsequently seized by customs authorities. When the case went before the United States Court of Appeals, it was the decision of Justice Augustus Hand that the "importation, sale, or carriage of things by mail which might legally be employed by conscientious and competent physicians for the purpose of saving life or promoting the well-being of their patients is to be permitted."

Two years later in 1938 the courts of Massachusetts held that it was illegal for doctors to dispense contraceptives at clinics, regardless of their purpose in protecting the health of patients—and it was illegal even to teach medical students the methods of birth control. It was not until 1966 that this law was changed, legalizing the distribution of birth control devices and allowing instruction to patients and physicians alike in birth control procedures.

In spite of all the various types of methods used in modern times to control or prevent conception, none proved to be 100 percent effective until 1960, when the first oral contraceptive became available.

Throughout history war, pestilence, and famine have exerted their influences to limit human population, which has now reached approximately 3½ billion. We have come to a time in man's social evolution when, contrary to Malthus' pessimistic expectations, man is capable of understanding the implications of unlimited population. Moreover, he has now the means and the conviction to apply them for the sake of his individual and collective well-being—possibly his very survival.

2

The "Best" Birth Control Method

Until recent years the methods of birth control may have been numerous, but most were relatively ineffective, shrouded in folklore, and handed down in whispers from mother to daughter or midwife to wife. Today, with the advent of much more effective and scientifically proven techniques, every person of reproductive age throughout the world can have an understanding of all current contraceptive methods—their advantages, disadvantages, safety, degree of effectiveness, suitability, and relative convenience.

The method chosen by one couple may not be desirable for another. The cultural, educational, psychological, and religious background of each individual and couple are important factors in the decision of which method is best for them. The physician too will consider these elements when giving his recommendation.

Any method is better than none, but the best is one that will be employed 100 percent of the time. No matter how effective any method may be proven clinically, it will not be successful for the person who harbors a secret fear or dislike of it, or who finds it difficult to apply.

Of all the current methods in the following list, oral contraceptives, vaginal diaphragms, and intrauterine devices are the most commonly used—with the possible exception of rhythm.

>   Cervical cap
>   "Combined" methods
>   Condom
>   Diaphragm with jelly or cream
>   Douche
>   Female sterilization
>   Intrauterine devices
>   Jelly, cream, or aerosol foam alone
>   Male sterilization
>   Oral contraceptives
>   Rhythm, calendar
>   Rhythm, temperature
>   Sponge and foam
>   Sponge and tampons with household spermatocides
>   Suppositories
>   Withdrawal (coitus interruptus and coitus reservatus)

The methods of contraception available today are a far cry from the repugnant substances and painful devices that woman for centuries was forced to employ in her futile efforts to avoid continuous pregnancy, with resulting malnutrition and high risk of premature death.

No longer a virtual slave or chattel whose reproductive faculty lies at the mercy of man, twentieth-century woman comes into the control of her fertility as she rises toward social equality. It can even be argued that her easy control of effective means of birth prevention is the greatest step toward her achieving a single standard of sexual morality.

Dr. Mary S. Calderone, executive director of SIECUS (Sex Information and Education Council of the U.S.), has written in the preface to *Manual of Contraceptive Practice:* "*The right of a woman in the matter of her own body should once and for all be recognized as a right in its own right.*"

3

Oral Contraceptives

The discovery of almost 100 percent effective birth control pills in the middle of the twentieth century has made medical history. It has already changed sexual mores, affected religious bias against birth control, and may be the single most important weapon in man's growing determination to control his numbers.

In 1940 Dr. Gregory Pincus published a paper suggesting that a female sex hormone could be used to prevent ovulation. In 1952 he and Dr. John Rock tried this hormone on a group of women volunteers. The results were encouraging. In 1956 a compound similar to a female hormone and derived from the wild Mexican yam was synthesized and proved to be cheaper and more effective—in fact, effective enough to warrant field trials on an international scale. By 1960 the Food and Drug Administration granted its approval for the first birth control pill to be made available for the American public.

The timely arrival of The Pill, as it came to be called, practically coincided with the realization around the world of the problems posed by the population explosion. Since the world population has been increasing at an estimated 170,000 births per day, or about one million people every six days, more and more governments are launching programs to limit their population growth in an effort to improve their countries' social and economic standards.

THE BIOLOGY OF CONCEPTION

The oral contraceptives achieve fertility control by preventing or suppressing ovulation. To understand how they work, one must first have an understanding of the conceptive process and ovulation.

The beginning of life in all mammals is the fertilization of the female egg or ovum by the sperm of the male. Deep in the pelvic cavity of a woman are two ovaries where eggs or ova are formed—from puberty to menopause. Hundreds of thousands of eggs are contained in the ovaries but only one ripens each month to the point where it can be fertilized.

Billions of sperm are produced in the human testes in the course of man's even longer fertile period, but only one, rarely two, can fertilize an egg at any one time. No one knows whether that particular sperm succeeds by chance or has some hitherto undiscovered properties which make it victorious.

Is this selectivity of a few among millions of possible matings of inheritance-laden sex cells an example of nature's wastefulness or some sort of guarantee that the strongest or best cells will be used to create future generations?

Ovulation is the release or rupture of a female egg cell from a mature egg follicle. It occurs painlessly (usually) and with little fanfare, somewhere in the middle of the menstrual cycle. This release of the egg depends primarily on hormonal influences generated from the pituitary gland located at the base of the brain and from the ovaries themselves. Ovulation can result in fertilization and conception within a three-day period only. And, of course, without ovulation there can be no conception.

HOW THE PILL WORKS

The current synthetic oral contraceptives act in very much the same way as estrogen and progesterone, two types of natural ovarian hormones (which are responsible for the absence of ovulation during pregnancy). These hormones inhibit the pituitary gland in its secretion of the hormones necessary for ovulation.

The Pill has two other contraceptive mechanisms in addition to its main function in preventing ovulation. It makes the cervical mucus act as a barrier to sperm; instead of becoming watery and receptive to sperm at the middle of the cycle, the mucus remains thick so sperm cells cannot penetrate. The Pill also acts on the endometrium (lining of the uterus) in such a manner to render it unfavorable for the implantation of a fertilized egg. It produces changes in the endometrium similar to those occurring in pregnancy.

TWO TYPES OF CONTRACEPTIVE PILLS

The classic contraceptive pill, administered from Day 5 to Day 25 of the menstrual cycle, is comprised of an estrogen-progestogen *combination*. Many variations have been developed since the first formulation of Drs. Pincus and Rock, all of which have proven virtually 100 percent effective.

A second generation of contraceptive pills referred to as *sequential* soon became available. In sequential therapy estrogens are administered from Day 5 to Day 25, and a progestogen is added from Day 21 to Day 25 of the menstrual cycle. In many cases this regimen proved just as effective and the onset of menstruation just as regular as with the combination pill, while the incidence of side effects was somewhat reduced. However, statistics indicate the sequential pill to be slightly less effective than the combination pill—the pregnancy rate on sequential treatment is 2 percent (2 failures per 100 woman-years of use) and 0.1 percent on combined treatment.

HOW CONTRACEPTIVE PILLS ARE TAKEN

Contraceptive pills are started after a menstrual period. The first day of menstrual bleeding is labeled Day 1. The first pill is taken on Day 5, whether or not the menstrual flow has stopped. A pill is taken every succeeding day for a total of twenty or twenty-one days, depending on the particular medication being used. The next menstrual period usually occurs one to seven days after the last pill in the series has been taken.

The next series of pills, and each succeeding series, is taken in a similar manner. When the menstrual period occurs after a course of pills, the first day of menstrual bleeding is again labeled Day 1. The taking of the pills again starts on Day 5 and continues on a once-a-day basis for the period prescribed.*

Physicians suggest that the pill be taken at the same time every day. If the pills are omitted, ovulation and pregnancy may result—the incidence of pregnancy increases proportionately to the number of missed pills. Omission of one or more pills also increases the incidence of spotting or bleeding.

If a scheduled pill is omitted, it should be taken any time during the next twenty-four hours and the next pill taken at the regular time.

If menstrual bleeding does not occur by the seventh day after taking the last pill in the series, the next series of pills should be started on that day without waiting for menstruation to start.

If spotting (slight brownish discharge) or breakthrough bleeding (menstrual flow) occurs during the course of medication, the physician should be consulted for further advice.

* A more recent type of birth control tablet, also started on Day 5, is taken for three weeks, discontinued for one week, and resumed for three weeks, regardless of the exact day menstruation begins.

ADVANTAGES OF THE PILL

The oral contraceptive is the most reliable and efficient method of birth control yet developed. If the medication is taken precisely as prescribed, it will be 99.9 percent effective.

The Pill has many practical attributes—it is simple to use, portable, and not costly. (Researchers are hard at work in an effort to bring the cost down to a few cents per pill.) For the first time a contraceptive method has been separated in time and place from the sexual act itself, allowing for much more spontaneity and contributing to the peace of mind necessary to achieve the ultimate success in sexual relationships.

Besides improving the psychological aspects of sex, The Pill has proven its effectiveness in improving many physical problems. It can make irregular periods become more regular; it can allow for advancing or retarding a menstrual period; it is sometimes very effective in preventing certain kinds of menstrual cramps and instances of premenstrual tension or depression; it can be of great benefit to certain people with acne, and it can help breast development in flat-chested women.

Oral contraceptives are of value in the older woman approaching menopause, for they prevent the irregular and often delayed menstrual periods which so frequently accompany the menopause and lead to anxiety about pregnancy. They also are effective in preventing or relieving hot flushes and other physical and emotional symptoms frequently characterizing the menopause.

DISADVANTAGES OF THE PILL

Some women have found that taking oral contraceptives has produced such unpleasant side effects that they have discontinued their use. Among the complaints listed are nausea, vomiting, breast tenderness or fullness, pelvic pain, headache, dizziness, acne, facial pigmentation, a tendency to gain weight, nervousness, depression, loss of scalp hair, excessive growth of body hair, increased libido, and decreased libido.

In addition, some women have experienced breakthrough bleeding or spotting, absence of menstruation, or lighter or heavier menstrual flow than usual. Fluid retention, usually mild, is also noted occasionally.

None of these signs and symptoms presents a serious medical problem. Many can be reduced considerably and others may be eliminated entirely. Most of these complaints are noted in the first months of therapy, after which side effects seem to disappear. Many physicians feel that part of the reason for the sometimes difficult adjustment to the very first series of pills may be psychological rather than physical. Even placebos (inert substances) have resulted in many similar symptoms.

The loss of scalp hair and excessive growth of body hair will disappear when medication is stopped. The nausea and vomiting may sometimes be alleviated by taking the medication after the evening meal, or if that is inconvenient, by taking an antacid or milk along with the pill. Breakthrough bleeding can often be terminated by doubling the dose of the medication for a few days. Diuretic tablets can be of help in curtailing or preventing excessive fluid accumulation resulting from the pills.

COMMON CONCERNS ABOUT SAFETY

People who have become pregnant despite taking The Pill (in almost all instances the pills had not been taken as prescribed) have had normal pregnancies and have delivered normal babies. No chromosomal abnormalities have been found either in experimental animals or in human infants. In fact, progesterone is one of the treatments given to prevent spontaneous abortion. Furthermore, future fertility is not endangered—it may even be enhanced—following long use of The Pill.

Nevertheless, The Pill is not innocuous enough to be taken

except upon a physician's advice and supervision. There is evidence to suggest that The Pill somewhat increases the risk of a woman's developing thrombophlebitis and/or pulmonary embolism. However, these conditions are still more common during and immediately after pregnancy. A woman who has previously had phlebitis or pulmonary embolism is usually not given oral contraceptives because they might be held responsible for a recurrence. Similarly, women with certain kinds of liver disease are often advised against taking The Pill. It may also be hazardous to women suffering from migraines or those who have a history of cancer of the breast, uterus, or ovaries.

To date, there has been no evidence that cancer, whether of the breast, uterus, ovaries, cervix, or other sites, has resulted from prolonged use of oral contraceptives. The Federal Government and drug manufacturers have been and are continuing to study any possible cause-and-effect relationship which may manifest itself after an increasing number of years.

4

Intrauterine Devices

The recently developed intrauterine device, or IUD, is proving to be an extremely popular method of contraception, second only to the oral contraceptives in effectiveness. It is, however, recommended most frequently for women who have already produced a child or have been pregnant.

The IUD, which today is made in a variety of shapes, was first suggested in a 1929 publication by Ernst Grafenberg, a German gynecologist. It was he who made the discovery that placing and leaving a ring within the uterus had a contraceptive effect. The original Grafenberg ring was made of silver wire and had the disadvantage of requiring a medical procedure (dilatation of the cervix) before it could be inserted. Because of the manner of insertion and because a number of cases of pelvic infection followed insertion, the IUD met with disfavor in the United States.

In the 1940's Israeli and Japanese scientists wrote of their work with the IUD, but it was not until the early 1950's with the utilization of plastics that general interest was renewed in IUDs—they could be mass-produced at a cost of ½¢ apiece. In 1959 an article in the *American Journal of Obstetrics and Gynecology* by Dr. Willi Oppenheimer of Israel reawakened America's interest in this method of contraception.

HOW THE IUD WORKS

The IUD poses one of the great mysteries of gynecology today. There are many theories about why the presence of a foreign body (such as an IUD) in the uterus prevents conception, but no one really knows what makes it work. The normal passage of sperm through the cervix does not seem affected nor does the IUD appear to interfere with ovulation.

The most popular theory is that the use of an IUD increases the speed with which the fertilized ovum travels through the fallopian tube, so that it arrives in the uterus before the ovum is ready to be implanted—or maybe the uterus is not yet prepared for implantation.

Experiments with monkeys have indicated that an IUD hurries the simian ovum through the tube in about three hours, a trip that normally would take three days.

DIFFERENT TYPES OF IUDS

The new intrauterine devices come in many shapes and, for the most part, are made of a flexible plastic. The one characteristic that they all share is that they can be straightened to permit insertion through the narrow canal of the undilated cervix, and once inside the uterus, they can return to their original form.

Named for their inventors, the three most commonly used IUDs are the Lippes loop, the Margulies spiral, and the Birnberg bow. Other IUDs include the Hall-Stone steel ring, the Nash plastic "earring" device, and the Marco-Nash plastic "harp."

HOW IUDS ARE PUT INTO PLACE

The pliable material of the various devices is stretched and threaded into a small introducer that resembles a soda straw. Then, with an instrument similar to a knitting needle, the device in the introducer is pushed painlessly into the uterus where it resumes its initial shape.

Although an IUD can be inserted on any day of the menstrual cycle, either of the two last days of menstruation is considered the best time because insertion is easier then and there is no danger of placing a device into a pregnant uterus.

ADVANTAGES OF THE IUD

The greatest advantage of an intrauterine device is that it remains in place for an indefinite period and there is no need for further contraceptive precautions. The couple has the added advantage of being unaware of the presence of the device.

The freedom from having to take almost daily medication or having to use other birth control methods at the time of intercourse—plus the inexpensiveness of the IUD itself—makes this method of contraception an appealing one to many women.

DISADVANTAGES OF THE IUD

A certain percentage of women wearing an intrauterine device experience some problem soon after insertion. One of the commonest problems is the expulsion of the device from the uterus. If expulsion is going to occur, it usually happens during the first, second, or third menstrual period. Physicians recommend one reinsertion following expulsion. If the device is retained longer, it most likely will be retained for years. For a few months after insertion menstrual flow tends to be heavier and longer.

Other possible complications of the IUD include cramps, backache, and bleeding between menstrual periods. Occasionally there is a discharge severe enough to require wearing a sanitary napkin or tampon. A very small number of women develop pelvic inflammatory disease after insertion of an IUD. The most serious complication is perforation of the uterus, but this generally occurs when the device has been inserted within five weeks after delivery.

Two to three percent of IUD users become pregnant during the first year following insertion. While the IUD is not quite as effective as The Pill, it is on a par with the diaphragm or condom used properly.

5

Other Effective Birth Control Methods

There are a number of mechanical and chemical methods of contraception which have been widely practiced for decades and are still in popular use today.

In the past decade or so there have been some innovations in materials and chemicals that have improved the efficiency of these birth control methods. However, despite their improved efficiency, The Pill and the IUD have proven even more reliable.

DIAPHRAGM

Among married women the vaginal diaphragm was the most popular form of contraception until The Pill came on the market, and is still the method of choice of many women who cannot or do not want to take oral contraceptives.

A thin rubber dome mounted on a rubber-covered wire spring, the diaphragm comes in various shapes. One recent model allows curving of the spring, enabling the physician to fit a woman whose anatomical variation previously made it impossible for her to be fitted for a diaphragm. This improvement in design also enables her to insert it with greater reliability.

Of great importance is the proper fitting of a diaphragm by a qualified physician. It forms a partition whose edges stretch the elastic vaginal walls to such a degree that sperm cannot pass around it into the cervical opening. Extra protection is afforded by the application of a spermatocidal jelly or cream on both sides of the diaphragm before insertion.

Every woman fitted for a diaphragm is measured by a group of fitting rings whose range runs in half-sizes from 50 to 105 millimeters in diameter. The most commonly used size is 75, with the majority of women requiring sizes 65 to 90.

Anyone who uses a diaphragm should have its size checked once a year, as well as after having a baby, a miscarriage, a gynecological operation, or a weight gain or loss of ten pounds or more.

A popular misconception among brides-to-be is that there must be a delay of weeks or months after marriage before a diaphragm can be fitted. The truth of the matter is that diaphragms can be, and frequently are, fitted even when the hymen is intact by means of gentle stretching by the doctor and later by the prospective bride. If a woman can use even the smallest size vaginal tampon, she can accommodate a diaphragm with little difficulty. A recently married woman whose vagina has been stretched by intercourse may require a larger size diaphragm than the one originally fitted for her.

For maximal safety a diaphragm must be fitted properly, inserted properly, and not removed for at least six hours after sexual relations. If intercourse takes place again within the six-hour period, the diaphragm should be left in place and more jelly or cream inserted with the applicator per instructions from the physician. The diaphragm should not be removed in less than six hours after the last ejaculation. Douching, if desired, should not be done until it is safe to remove the diaphragm.

The recent Johnson and Masters studies of female sexual response have accounted for the occasional failures of the properly inserted diaphragm. These studies have demonstrated that the more vigorous the movements during intercourse, the greater variety of positions, and the more frequent the entries, the greater the risk of the diaphragm's slipping from its proper position with resulting penetration of the penis or sperm beyond the rim of the diaphragm.

CERVICAL CAP

The cervical cap, a device which fits the cervix the way a thimble fits the thumb, was invented in 1860 by a New York physician, E.B. Foote. Dr. Foote's cervical cap soon fell into oblivion and in 1908 the modern cervical cap was developed by a Viennese gynecologist, Dr. Karl Kafka.

This method of birth control requires the services of a physician and is not commonly used in the United States except in the South. The cervical cap, however, is widely used in England and Central Europe. For reasons which have yet to be evaluated, American women, both private and clinic patients, have much greater difficulty in mastering the cap technique than European women, who find it only very slightly more difficult to learn than the diaphragm technique.

There are two basic types of cervical caps—those made of soft, pliable rubber which are generally prescribed in England, and the firm cervical caps which were previously made of resin, celluloid, and metals but today are made of lucite, a clear plastic. Because the soft rubber caps are more difficult to insert and to remove than the diaphragm and because they can be worn for only twenty-four hours at a time, most American gynecologists favor the use of the firm cervical cap which can be worn for much longer periods.

The lucite cervical cap is fitted by the physician and inserted initially after a menstrual period. It can remain in position for a number of days up until the next menstrual period. At this time the cap should be removed. If the menstrual period should start unexpectedly while the cap is in place, the flow can escape, indicating the cap should then be removed.

The narrow, smooth-edged rim of the lucite cap facilitates the insertion and removal of the cap by the woman herself. Once she has mastered the cap technique and can easily remove and reinsert the cap every few days, the use of a spermatocidal cream or jelly inside the cap provides additional contraceptive protection. The lucite may become discolored after prolonged use, but the same cap can be used for at least a two-year period.

The cervical cap is frequently prescribed for women who cannot use a diaphragm for anatomical or other reasons, or for the rare occasion when either wife or husband may be allergic to rubber. When a diaphragm cannot be fitted for a bride-to-be because of an intact hymen, a small cervical cap can usually be fitted without pain or injury.

The advantages of the cervical cap are that it offers prolonged protection and that, like The Pill and the IUD, it separates the decision to use contraception from the sexual act.

The main disadvantage of the cervical cap is that its technique is more difficult to perfect than that of the diaphragm. Most women can learn how to remove the cap in one or two sessions, but many are unable to learn self-insertion, which makes a monthly visit to the physician necessary. For those who require assistance for both insertion and removal, two monthly visits would be needed.

The contraceptive effectiveness of the cervical cap is approximately the same as that of the proper use of the diaphragm-and-jelly technique and condoms.

CONDOM

The condom is a very thin sheath or cover that is placed over the penis just before coitus to prevent conception. It is the most widely used mechanical contraceptive in the United States and throughout the world.

The majority of condoms on the market today are made of rubber. In recent years there has been a renewed interest in "skin" condoms made from sheep's intestine, which cost about three times the price of inexpensive rubber sheaths. Considered an item for the luxury market, skin condoms are reputed to interfere less with sexual enjoyment than rubber ones because animal membrane is a better conductor of heat than rubber and more readily transmits tactile sensations.

Since the Renaissance period, condoms have been associated with illicit sex and the avoidance of venereal disease, and today remain the method of choice in sexual relations of a casual or transitory nature. Because of its identification with "unclean" sex, there has been a reluctance among married couples to use this method. Nevertheless, in actual fact, the condom is one of the most effective methods of birth control available today.

The condom is recommended by physicians to married couples in many situations. In cases of vaginitis caused by *Trichomonas vaginalis* the use of condoms prevents reinfestation by the husband, who may harbor the parasite in his urethra or under the foreskin. The condom may be indicated when a woman has an anatomical variation that does not permit the fitting and use of a diaphragm, or it may be prescribed for newlyweds, or after childbirth until the vaginal muscles regain sufficient tone to allow satisfactory use of a diaphragm. The condom is also used temporarily while another contraceptive technique (such as cervical cap or diaphragm) is being learned.

For those women who prefer their husbands to take the responsibility for contraception and for those men who find it important psychologically to assume that responsibility, the condom is the perfect contraceptive agent. It is also reassuring to those couples who want evidence immediately following intercourse that they have been successfully protected. Some couples who generally use other methods use condoms for coitus during menstruation. Some men with premature ejaculation find condoms decrease sexual sensation, enabling them to have prolonged intercourse.

A failure can occur if a condom breaks or slips off at

withdrawal. For this reason, many physicians suggest that the condom should be used in conjunction with a vaginal jelly or cream.

"COMBINED" METHODS

It is quite apparent that for any couple whose sexual satisfaction demands even greater reassurance of contraceptive protection many methods can be combined, such as 1) condom, vaginal spermatocidal jelly or cream, and rhythm; 2) diaphragm, cervical cap, or IUD and rhythm; 3) condom and diaphragm; and 4) condom, rhythm, and diaphragm or cervical cap.

WITHDRAWAL

Withdrawal, the oldest method of birth control, is possibly the most widely used method today. It is referred to in many ways and by many names, among them *coitus interruptus*,* *coitus incompletus*, "taking care," and "being careful." It is also called onanism after Onan, son of Judah, whose practice of withdrawal is described in Genesis 38:9. "But Onan, knowing that the seed would not count as his, let it go to waste whenever he joined with his brother's wife, so as not to provide offspring for his brother."

In this method a man withdraws his erect penis from the woman's vagina when he feels ejaculation to be imminent, and ejaculates outside the woman's body. Safe withdrawal requires not only control on the man's part but a true awareness in advance of just when ejaculation is about to occur.

---

* Two varieties of coitus interruptus have found a following at different times and places. One referred to as *coitus saxonicus* is a method in which normal intercourse takes place but upon the imminent male orgasm, the woman compresses the base of the penis with her fingers, preventing the outflow of sperm, most of which is then ejaculated into the male bladder.

The other variety is called *coitus reservatus* or Karezza. This method requires a high degree of control and proficiency, for the point of climax is approached to such a degree (and often many times) that erection gradually subsides without ejaculation ever taking place.

For the man who is strongly motivated to protect his partner from pregnancy and can practice withdrawal correctly, it is a very effective contraceptive method. However, not all men ejaculate in one forceful spurt—perhaps as many as fifty percent do not. These latter may expel semen intermittently or slowly, and may not be able to tell the exact moment before semen starts to escape. Even one drop of semen, containing up to six million sperm, can be responsible for fertilization.

Sperm may enter the vagina under a number of different circumstances, even though intercourse has been interrupted. A drop of semen may escape before ejaculation; a man may be unable for many reasons to withdraw in time; ejaculation too close to the external sexual organs of the woman may enable sperm to migrate into the vagina. Couples, married or unmarried, who indulge in certain kinds of petting or rely on intercourse between the labia or between the thighs, run some risk of pregnancy, contrary to popular belief. There are cases recorded of women who, in spite of an intact hymen, became pregnant after participating in this type of sexual activity. (Many people are not aware that sperm possess considerable motility, and that if semen is deposited between the labia, there may be sufficient moisture for the sperm to remain alive and motile. Semen, once having dried, is not capable of causing fertilization.)

Withdrawal can be an effective birth control method for basically two types of men—those who have already used it successfully for five to ten years and young men belonging to that group who ejaculate all at once and who have learned how to achieve a prolonged preejaculatory period. (Dr. Alfred C. Kinsey's studies have shown that about fifty percent of all men either reach orgasm within two to five minutes or have a premature ejaculation and therefore have greater difficulty using the withdrawal method than the other fifty percent of men for whom intercourse usually may last five to twenty minutes.) For those men who ejaculate in several stages and still desire to practice withdrawal, physicians advise interrupting intercourse every time an ejaculation is about to occur, drying the tip of the penis and the urethral opening carefully with a handkerchief or towel before continuing.

Many couples have attributed lack of sexual enjoyment or satisfaction and even frigidity and impotence to repeated use of coitus interruptus. Although there is no evidence that withdrawal leads to any physical harm in either men or women, another method of contraception should be selected if withdrawal creates any psychological problems.

Certainly as an occasional method to be used in an "emergency," withdrawal will continue to be relied on as far better than no method at all.

6

Less Effective Birth Control Methods

Before the widespread use of The Pill, married American women were having almost twenty percent more children than they wanted, largely due to improper application of birth control methods, or to imperfections in the methods themselves. In other words, one child in every five (on the average) could be said to have been unwanted, or at least unplanned for.

Spacing one's children and limiting their number affect every phase of family life from maternal, fetal, and infant nutrition to interpersonal and sexual relationships. For a happier and healthier life a woman should not base her choice of a birth control method on old-wives' tales, personal theories, or product advertising, but on the best information currently available and on the advice of a physician.

CHEMICAL CONTRACEPTIVES USED ALONE

Since 1950 there have been concerted scientific efforts to eliminate the need for a mechanical barrier (a vaginal diaphragm) by replacing it with one of the newer chemical barriers referred to as intravaginal chemical contraceptive agents. These chemicals are designed to be used alone and to destroy sperm instantaneously upon contact.

There are several types of intravaginal chemical contraceptives available, including vaginal creams and jellies, aerosol foams, foam tablets, and vaginal suppositories. Of these, aerosol foams have been shown to be the most effective and have seemed to be more acceptable to most women because of relative lack of irritating effects and minimal vaginal leakage. Direct observation and color photography studies have demonstrated that the aerosol foam spreads over the vaginal walls and cervical canal areas somewhat better than the non-foaming intravaginal jellies and creams. Foam tablets and vaginal suppositories have not found as wide an acceptance.

Aerosol foam works on the same principle as jel or cream alone, except that it is packaged under pressure and is released as foam. Before using the aerosol foam the bottle should be shaken. Then the plastic syringe-like introducer should be fitted to the top of the bottle, thereby forcing the foam into the introducer. Within one hour before intercourse, the loaded plastic introducer should be inserted into the vagina and the plunger pushed to deliver the foam to the deeper part of the vagina. If more than an hour passes before having intercourse, another dose of the contraceptive agent should be inserted. A dose should be used each time before having sex relations.

After insertion of the contraceptive chemical agent, one should not get up or walk around. If it has been necessary to do so, then another applicatorful must be injected before coitus. Douching, if desired, should not be done until at least six hours after the last ejaculation.

The advantages of chemical contraceptives alone are that

they are easy to use, do not require the services of a physician or any special care, and are widely available without a prescription. In addition, many couples find their sex relations more satisfactory without the presence of a mechanical device.

None of the intravaginal chemical contraceptives is yet as effective as the diaphragm, condom, or cervical cap, but this newer type of birth control is about as protective as the rhythm method based on the thermometer.

RHYTHM

The only method of birth control (other than complete continence) permissible for centuries to followers of the Roman Catholic religion,* the rhythm technique, is based on the assumption that if a woman could know the exact day each month on which her ovum is produced, she could avoid intercourse on certain specified days.

The rhythm system is not applicable to about one-sixth of the female population because their menstrual cycles are too irregular. Even among women with regular menstrual periods, there is a great variation of the fertile period, so the rhythm method has a high failure rate. According to Dr. John Rock, American gynecologist famous for his work on family and population planning, ovulation occurs most dependably *about* fourteen days before Day 1 of the *following* menstruation. But the fertile period can fall anywhere from the eighth to the nineteenth day of a woman's cycle. Many gynecologists feel that a woman's only "safe period" is from the twentieth day of the menstrual cycle through menstruation and until the fifth day of the following menstrual period.

There are two ways by which a woman's fertile period may be more or less accurately estimated—by using the

* The first relaxation of the Church's ban on birth control came in November 1968 when the Roman Catholic Church of France declared: "Contraception can never be good. It is always a disorder, but this disorder is not always guilty." According to this declaration, adopted by 120 French bishops, each believer is to decide whether contraceptives would be sinful in his or her case.

calendar to keep track of the exact dates of the first days of the menstrual period for at least eight months, and by taking and charting her temperature the first thing every morning (basal body temperature) for at least two or three months. Intercourse must be restricted to perhaps the last ten or eleven days of the cycle or after the basal body temperature is elevated for three successive mornings. After a woman has given birth, it may take quite some time for the menstrual cycles to assume a regular pattern; hence, her basal body temperature during this period will not be a reliable guide to ovulation. A woman can become pregnant right after having a baby, even before menstruating again.

The diaphragm-and-jelly method of contraception as well as the condom have been shown to be two to three times as dependable as rhythm. The rhythm method might be more effective at some future date, were an easy and reliable test to indicate that ovulation was about to occur, or if a simple medication could reliably induce ovulation at a predictable time. Research on this problem is in progress at this writing in various parts of the world.

SPONGE AND FOAM

The sponge and foam method of contraception, though not new, is still popular with many women who have used it successfully. In this method the woman inserts into her vagina a small, soft sponge (one manufactured for this purpose, a rounded sea sponge, or a flat piece of rubber or plastic sponge). This is moistened with water and then impregnated with a sperm-killing powder or liquid. (If powder is used, it should be sprinkled a few times on each side of the sponge; if liquid is used, the sponge should be held flat against the bottle, which is turned quickly upside down once on each side of the sponge.)

By gentle kneading and squeezing of the sponge, the powder or liquid begins to form foam. The sponge is then pushed into the vagina as far back as possible. Its total foaming power does not develop until the movements of intercourse generate the foam. This reserve of foaming power is supposed to enable a couple to have sexual relations up to six hours after the sponge has been inserted. If intercourse is repeated, then an additional, smaller sponge prepared the same way is inserted. One or both sponges must remain in place until at least six hours after the last ejaculation. Douching, if desired, should not be done until after the same interval. The sponge may be removed by a string which has been previously attached to it, or by the fingers.

Sponge and foam is one of the least expensive birth control methods available and affords a generally satisfactory degree of protection. However, its effectiveness is not on a par with that of the diaphragm and jelly, or even of aerosol foams, creams, or jellies used alone. For many women the sponge and foam method is too messy and lacking in esthetic appeal.

SPONGES AND TAMPONS WITH HOUSEHOLD SPERMATOCIDES

Through the ages women have prepared various types of homemade tampons to be used as contraceptives. Today in remote areas where commercial contraceptives are not available, women still resort to a "do-it-yourself" type of birth control.

The ideal material for this type of contraceptive device is either a sea sponge or a piece of rubber or plastic sponge. Vaginal barriers have also been made of wool or cotton. Before insertion the sponge or tampon is saturated with a sperm-killing liquid, such as a combination of vinegar and lemon juice, or a solution of common table salt. However, vinegar and especially salt can be irritating to the vaginal membranes. Even plain water, which has some sperm-killing action on contact, has been used to saturate these vaginal tampons.

Most authorities question the contraceptive effectiveness of this method and these materials. The best that can be said of them is that they may be better than no method at all.

BREASTFEEDING (LACTATION)

It has long been believed throughout the world that new mothers have a built-in protection against conception for as long as they breastfeed their babies. While it is true that lactation usually delays the onset of menstruation, there is a slight but definite risk of pregnancy (about five percent), even in the absence of menstrual flow. Ovulation can occur about two weeks before the first postdelivery period, and if fertilization takes place at this time, no period will precede the following pregnancy. Therefore, women who wish to be maximally protected against becoming pregnant so soon after giving birth should seek and be given advice about effective measures of birth control as soon as they resume sexual intercourse.

DOUCHING

The belief persists that douching is an effective preventative against pregnancy, as well as a prophylaxis against venereal disease. In actual fact, douching is not very effective, if indeed, it has any contraceptive effect at all—for within a few seconds after ejaculation, sperm are already in the mucus covering the cervical opening, from where they have easy access to the uterine cavity. Caustic douches have actually caused harm to the sensitive vaginal tissues. There are many other chemicals, either manufactured or homemade, that may be harmless, but like douches of carbonated drinks, offer no more protection against conception than plain or soapy water. If a douche is used within the first six hours after intercourse when any vaginal contraceptive method has been employed, it may remove an effective barrier, and hence, *favor* the chances of conception.

7

Sterilization

Of all the modern techniques devised to prevent pregnancy, sterilization by surgery has probably been the most misunderstood and least appreciated until recent years. Frequently referred to as "permanent" contraception, surgical sterilization can, in some cases in both sexes, be reversed by a second operation.

According to the Association for Voluntary Sterilization, there are about 2,000,000 living Americans who have undergone voluntary sterilization. Each year more than 100,000 people are choosing to have it performed and the numbers are constantly increasing. Women account for approximately sixty percent of voluntary sterilizations, men approximately forty percent. Those who arrange to be sterilized come from all walks of life and from varying economic and religious backgrounds.

For those families in which further pregnancies constitute a threat to the physical or mental well-being of the mother, or jeopardize the social or economic life of the entire family, sterilization offers a relatively simple solution to a seemingly hopeless predicament.

SURGICAL PROCEDURES FOR WOMEN

The method of choice for female sterilization is the removal of sections from both fallopian tubes—bilateral subtotal salpingectomy*—which can be done within twelve to forty-eight hours after childbirth. (This procedure has even been performed while the woman is still in the delivery room under anesthesia.) Or it may be done as an elective operation at a time not related to pregnancy. If it is done following delivery, the operation is easier on the woman and easier for the surgeon to perform. Sterilization does not generally require lengthening the five- or six-day postdelivery hospital stay. Therefore, there is a saving of time and money when the mother can avoid a second hospitalization.

In the Pomeroy method of bilateral *subtotal* salpingectomy a section of each tube is removed and the remaining ends are tied, the whole procedure usually taking about twenty minutes or less. Because of its simplicity and success, the Pomeroy technique has been one of the most popular methods throughout the years. A variation of the Pomeroy operation is the Madlener, in which the tubes are tied but not cut. There is also a technique for vaginal tubal sterilization, which requires a general anesthetic but avoids the need for making an abdominal incision. However, this procedure is surgically more difficult. None of these sterilization techniques affects normal menstruation or normal sexual response.

In bilateral *total* salpingectomy both fallopian tubes are removed entirely, and sometimes a part of the cornua of the uterus (where the tubes are attached) is also removed. This

* Salpingectomy means, literally, removal of (part of) the fallopian tube or salpinx. The term "tubal ligation" applies to the older and less successful procedure of merely tying the tubes, but now is also used to refer, broadly speaking, to ligation with resection.

operation is usually performed only in cases where there is tubal disease.

Hysterectomy and bilateral oophorectomy are two surgical procedures that result in 100 percent sterilization, although they are hardly ever performed for this express purpose. Hysterectomy, removal of the uterus, is a common operation generally performed on women past the childbearing years for a specific medical reason. Bilateral oophorectomy or female castration, removal of the ovaries, is performed only in the treatment of serious medical illnesses.

REVERSAL OF FEMALE STERILIZATION

Several operations have been devised and employed for restoring the continuity of the fallopian tubes. The two ends of each tube which have been tied in the sterilizing operation are reconnected, often by using a small polyethylene tube during the procedure to assure that the junction remains open.

Tubal patency, as proven by a Rubin test or a suitable X-ray procedure, is restored in approximately one-half of those women operated upon, although this in itself does not establish proof of fertility. In women who have undergone reversal of sterilization the pregnancy rate is lower than that of the general female population of comparable age.

NONSURGICAL STERILIZATION FOR WOMEN

Other methods of sterilization that do not require surgery have been and are in the process of being developed. The Hyams method is one in which the cornua (uterine openings to the tubes) are cauterized. However, this technique requires extensive and complicated follow-up procedures. Work is currently being done on a technique in which a metal clip is placed on the tube itself through an instrument inserted into the vagina and called a culdoscope. Until the nonsurgical methods have proven themselves, the great majority of female sterilizations will still be performed by an abdominal surgical procedure.

Radiation by means of X-rays or radium implants can result in complete ovarian destruction, and hence, sterilization. This is, however, usually a by-product of treatment undertaken for cancer.

SURGICAL STERILIZATION FOR MEN

Vas deferens resection, or vasectomy, is a surgical procedure performed on a man as a permanent method of contraception. However, like female sterilization, it can be reversed in many instances.

Originating above each testicle, the vas deferens is a long, small, thick-walled tube that serves as a passageway in the male genitourinary tract. It joins the duct of the seminal vesicle to form the ejaculatory duct, which empties into the prostatic urethra, and thence into the penis.

Vas resection, performed via a very small incision on either side of the scrotum, mechanically prevents sperm from traveling the length of the vas deferens to reach the penile urethra; thus sperm is retained within the male and cannot be ejaculated. Spermatogenesis continues at a normal rate, but the sperm cells are broken down and absorbed back into the system with no harmful effects. Male sterilization is a simple procedure that takes less than half an hour and can be done in a doctor's office. The man is usually able to return to work the day after the operation. Once the complete absence of sperm has been proven by a microscopic examination of ejaculated semen, assurance of sterility approaches 100 percent.

It is only in recent years that this operation has begun to be understood and accepted by the male population, with the result that it has been used increasingly by men willing to undertake responsibility for birth prevention. In the past many men equated vasectomy with castration or feared that such an operation would interfere with normal erection and ejaculation. In actual fact, neither the sexual drive nor potency is affected adversely in any way, and ejaculation occurs without appreciable diminution of the amount of seminal fluid. In many cases potency improves when the fear of conception is eliminated.

Still in the developmental stage is a new technique for male sterilization whereby a removable clip is used for clamping the vas deferens.

REVERSAL OF MALE STERILIZATION

Although it has been rare that a man's circumstances are so altered that he desires restoration of fertility, sterility has been successfully reversed surgically in at least two thirds to three quarters of such cases. The technique again involves bilateral scrotal incisions in which, as described in reversal of female sterilization, the severed ends of each vas deferens (like the fallopian tubes) are resewn together end to end. Proof of success can be predicted by postoperative semen analyses.

LEGAL ASPECTS OF STERILIZATION

Laws involving sterilization generally come under the jurisdiction of the states, and therefore, can vary from state to state. One has to be certain to distinguish laws pertaining to compulsory sterilization—broadly speaking, the duty of the state—and voluntary sterilization, the choice of the individual.

Compulsory sterilization in about twenty-seven states is permitted by law to be performed on inmates of state mental institutions under specified circumstances. Although permitted by law, very few compulsory sterilizations have actually been carried out.

Voluntary contraceptive sterilization is legal in all fifty states. In only two states—Connecticut and Utah—it is limited to reasons of "medical necessity." Before any sterilization operation is performed, the doctor will require the written consent of the person requesting sterilization and the spouse, if there be one. The statement also releases the surgeon of any and all responsibility for any complications that could possibly result from such a procedure. Usually two witnesses sign the statement, or if the physician prefers, it is notarized.

8

Contraception for Minors

The moral and medical aspects of sex are in the process of evolution and revolution. The "new morality" is having an all-too-direct effect on older children and teen-agers, whose widespread indulgence in sexual activities is reaping tragic results—a mounting number of forced marriages, illegitimate pregnancies, illegal abortions, and cases of venereal disease.

There has been a drop in the age of the first sexual experience, which today occurs frequently between twelve and sixteen years. The National Council on Illegitimacy recently reported that of the more than 250,000 women who bear illegitimate children in the United States every year, approximately 90,000 of these mothers are teen-agers. (In the past two decades the annual number of illegitimate births has more than doubled.) There are now 3 million children under eighteen born out of wedlock. Of the one million annual abortions and the 5,000–15,000 deaths from criminal abortions annually, one can estimate that teen-age girls comprise approximately one third of this number.

Of the 100,000 new cases of infectious syphilis diagnosed in the United States in one year, half are in the age group from ten to twenty-four years. One out of every thirty-five Americans in this age range has contracted either syphilis or gonorrhea. Gonorrhea attacks more than twice as many victims as syphilis.

THE NEED FOR SEX EDUCATION

As long as an individual under twenty-one is to be legally regarded a minor, no matter what the degree of his or her emotional maturity, the parents must take responsibility to see that their children are aware of the hazards, emotional and otherwise, of premarital sexual relations. The parents must also be prepared to help their children seek medical advice regarding birth—and disease—prevention.

Intransigence on the parents' part may have the consequence of breakdown in communication between child and parent. And this is perhaps the greatest barrier to the child's receiving proper guidance and medical assistance, if necessary.

In 1966 Katherine B. Oettinger, Chief of the Children's Bureau of the Department of Health, Education, and Welfare, made a statement in which she indicated that family planning services would be available to all who request them. This has become accepted policy in federally financed planned parenthood clinics and health department clinics. In addition, private physicians, many college student health services, and some hospital clinics are beginning to provide contraceptive advice and/or materials for single girls. In most instances parental consent is sought or required. A complete physical examination and often intensive individual counseling are undertaken before reaching any decisions as to contraceptive advice—for the mere dispensing of contraceptives to teenagers without an opportunity for psychological evaluation, sex education, and counseling could, with some justification, be accused of fostering promiscuity and substituting "diseased adults" for unwanted babies.

Whether or not sex education by parents, schools, religious advisors, physicians, or psychiatrists will have any influence in countering "the teen-age copulation explosion," at least the consequences of permissive sexual behavior can be held to a minimum by advocacy and application of birth- and disease-prevention methods. The World War II adage propounded to millions of American soldiers regarding sexual promiscuity was: "Don't . . . but if you must, be careful." American children of both sexes deserve at least as much consideration and cautionary counsel.

9

Contraception in the Future

The discovery that led to the development of The Pill—that *synthetic* hormones such as norethindrone and norethynodrel could be more powerful than the *natural* hormones—has spurred research into the development of other powerful synthetic hormones which might increase or decrease male or female fertility. These and other synthetic agents have already been applied in the fields of animal husbandry, insect control, and plant reproduction. Further experimentation in the laboratory, followed by trials in animals and finally in humans, gives high promise of still more effective, safer, and more easily applied systemic contraceptives.

For example, a new compound, chlormadinone, has already been synthesized and shown in clinical trials to be extremely effective in small daily doses. It has been called The Minipill and appears to work, not by preventing ovulation, but by altering the cervical mucus in such a way that it becomes hostile to sperm.

Also in the trial stage is the one-pill-a-month contraceptive, which consists of a long-acting estrogen combined with a short-acting progestogen. Similarly, a once-a-month injection of a long-acting estrogen-progestogen compound is under active investigation, as is a once-a-year injection of large amounts of long-acting hormones. Under development too is a capsule which, when implanted under the skin, could work for periods up to 900 days.

To remove all need for using any anticipatory contraceptive, concerted research efforts are being directed to finding a pill which is to be taken only *after* intercourse. It has variously been called the "morning-after pill," the "second-thoughts pill," and the "week-later pill." Such a pill would work by interfering with the implantation of the fertilized egg or causing it to be sloughed off shortly after implantation.

A contraceptive pill for the man is also under study—several compounds have already been shown to reversibly inhibit sperm formation without in any way interfering with a man's normal sex drive or potency. "The Male Pill" would probably be taken once a month.

The simplicity, safety, ease of administration, and availability at reasonable cost of these synthetic contraceptive chemicals will revolutionize marriage and sex in the future, for the problem of how to prevent children will be replaced by the headier decisions of whether and when to have them.

PART II

THE ABORTION REVOLUTION

10

Historical Viewpoints on Abortion

Induced abortion is one of the world's oldest ethical and legal issues. Today's opinions as to whether or not abortion should be legalized fluctuate between a traditional, dogmatic morality and a progressive, humane outlook, with many gradations separating the two points of view.

Throughout the centuries attitudes toward the deliberate interruption of pregnancy have varied from condemnation as the gravest of offenses to commendation in the interest of the general community. Written in the Code of the Assyrian Law Relating to Women (? 1500 B.C.) is the regulation: "If a woman of her own accord causes to fall what her womb holds, she shall be tried, convicted, and impaled upon a stake, and shall not be buried. If she dies in committing abortion upon herself, she shall be impaled upon a stake and shall not be buried."

The ancient Greeks viewed abortion far differently—they accepted it as a general practice. To Plato abortion was the solution for couples whom he considered too old for parenthood. Aristotle, aware even then of the dangers of overpopulation, regarded abortion as the best way of keeping the population within the numerical limits which he thought essential to the well-being of the community. It is a paradox that his definition of the three stages of development of the soul into the human body greatly influenced the literature of the Roman Catholic Church for centuries later. Aristotle initiated the concept that a fetus was endowed with vegetative life at conception, with an animal soul several days later, and finally with a rational soul on the 40th day of gestation for a male and on the 80th day of gestation for a female.

Abortion was practiced in Greece (and in Rome) for such other reasons as avoiding the shame of bearing an illegitimate child, avoiding the financial burden of rearing an unwanted child and, for many vain women, avoiding the ungainly appearance of the pregnant state.

The Pythagoreans, members of a mystic minority sect who preceded Plato and Aristotle, condemned abortion because of their ascetic attitude toward all sexual matters and their belief that the soul is infused into the body at the instant of conception. On the other hand, the Stoics denied the existence of a soul before birth, and a popular theory of the Hellenistic culture (in about the second century A.D.) held that infants were not considered human until they had partaken of human food.

It is thought that the anti-abortion doctrines of the Pythagoreans influenced the pledge against abortion in the Oath of Hippocrates, which states: "I will not give to a woman an abortive remedy." However, scholars feel that this attitude against abortion, which was not representative of general opinion in its times, is unrelated to the development of negative attitudes toward abortion in so-called modern times many centuries later.

THE ROMAN CATHOLIC VIEWPOINT

The early Christian Church is credited as being the source of the thesis that abortion is murder—a seemingly simple and direct interpretation of the Sixth Commandment, "Thou shalt not kill." The discussions and ecclesiastical debates that began in the third century—whether abortion is always murder or sometimes murder or sometimes not murder—have never abated. The Roman theologian Tertullian (AD. 230?), a leader of the Montanist sect, charged that abortion was murder, with the modification that murder occurred only if the fetus had developed to a certain stage at which it could be considered a living human being. Saint Augustine (A.D. 354–430), the great Christian theologian who ranks among the early Fathers of the Church, also differentiated between a "formed" and a "nonformed" fetus, and also between a "living" and a "not-yet-living" fetus. There were questions, too, of the fetus being "animated" or "nonanimated"—whether or not the fetus had already been imbued with a soul.

It was this question of exactly *when* the soul is introduced into the fetus that became a major theological issue for centuries, for the destruction of an animated fetus was a much graver sin than that of a nonanimated fetus and the penalties were much more severe. This distinction became a part of formalized Canon Law* about the middle of the twelfth century and later was incorporated into the common law of England.**

In the thirteenth century Gregory IX and Innocent III maintained the several-centuries-old view that in a clear dis-

---

* A collection of laws and regulations for the religious government of members of the Roman Catholic Church.

** The body of rules found in the written records of judges' decisions. American law is based on English common law, but it has been changed by legislation and by the courts.

tinction between formed and unformed fetuses, the killing of an unformed fetus was punishable by a fine only. However, in 1588 Sixtus V reinstated all previous rigid restrictions on abortion at any prenatal stage and added the penalty of excommunication even for advisors. This decree was slightly liberalized in 1591 by Gregory XIV, after which time the difference between animate and inanimate fetuses was never again introduced.

It was in 1869 that the Roman Catholic Church abolished the forty- and eighty-day theory of animation, and since that time, the generally accepted dogma is that the fetus is a human being from the instant of conception, and therefore, the gravity of the sin of abortion is the same no matter at what time it is committed. The Catholic Church today regards abortion as a Canon Law crime in its own right, apart from the crime of murder.

As a result of the Catholic Church's ban on *all* abortion, no Catholic hospital may be used to perform an abortion procedure, even for medical necessity, and no Catholic physician is allowed to perform such a procedure at a non-Catholic hospital. Catholic doctors are not even supposed to refer a Catholic patient to a Jewish or Protestant doctor for therapeutic abortion.

There is, however, one exception to the Church's prohibition of hospital abortion—the doctrine of "double effect." If the fetus should die as the indirect consequence of a procedure specifically designed to cure or save the life of the mother, no sin is committed. For example, in contrast to a 1902 ruling by a Congregation of the Holy Office which condemned any surgical treatment upon a fetus lodged fatally in a fallopian tube, the unofficial Church position since the 1940's has condoned operation for tubal pregnancy—since its purpose would be to save the life of the mother, the killing of the embryo being only an indirect and specifically unintended result. This principle of double effect would also apply if a hysterectomy for uterine cancer had to be done on a pregnant woman.

THE JEWISH VIEWPOINT

In contrast with Catholic theology, Judaism has never been concerned with the concept of soul and the timing of fetal "animation," nor does Jewish theology regard the fetus as a separate human entity, but as a part of the mother. Only when during the process of birth the child's head or the greater part of its body has emerged from the womb, is the baby referred to as a living soul. Even if an infant should die during the first thirty days after birth, no funeral service is conducted, as such a baby is regarded as not having been destined to live, its short survival considered merely an accident of nature.

According to the Mishnah (a section of the Talmud consisting of collected oral laws edited before A.D. 200), a woman having difficulty in giving birth is entitled to destroy, or have destroyed, her unborn child (embryotomy) in order to save her life. Later, in the eleventh century, Rashi, the classic Jewish commentator and Biblical interpreter, did not consider that taking the life of an unborn fetus was murder because, in his words, "Whatever has not come forth into the light of the world is not a human life [lit. 'soul']."

Moses ben Maimon, better known as Maimonides (1135–1204), the rabbi-philosopher who tried to harmonize Judaism with the teachings of Aristotle, codified the interpretations of these earlier authorities. In cases when pregnancy was a threat to the mother's life, he viewed the fetus "like a pursuer [intent on] killing her." After Maimonides, the Jewish attitude on abortion through the centuries has been based on *responsa*, written opinions of rabbis and teachers in answer to questions submitted by members of Jewish congregations.

According to Rabbi Immanuel Jakobovits'* comprehensive book, *Jewish Medical Ethics*, there are very few references to criminal abortion in Jewish religious literature before the twelfth century, when it was casually mentioned. Dr. Jakobo-

---

* Chief Rabbi of Great Britain.

vits states: "There is no reference to the subject in the codes, and even the responsa do not discuss it until the seventeenth century." He further declares that therapeutic abortions, which are generally sanctioned in Jewish law, are rarely mentioned in Jewish historical sources. "Yet," says Dr. Jakobovits, "there can be little doubt that Jewish physicians resorted to them, and particularly to embryotomy . . . whenever other methods to save the mother failed."

The three branches of Judaism—Orthodox, Conservative, and Reform—agree on their concepts regarding the origins of human life but disagree on certain points regarding the conditions that justify abortion. Orthodox rabbis argue that as long as the mother's life is not threatened by a pregnancy, the fetus cannot be aborted under any circumstances—that no one has the right to decide between a life and a life.

Since the beginning of the nineteenth century when the Reform movement began in Germany and later when the Conservative movement began in western Europe, therapeutic abortion has been approved in such conditions as threatened deafness, tuberculosis, and psychiatric illness in the mother. More recently, it has been approved when rubella (German measles) in the mother results in the strong likelihood that she will bear an abnormal child.

The basic outlook of the Jewish majority is that the life and health of the woman come before that of the fetus, and when medical necessity indicates an abortion, there are no religious regulations to overcome. In recent years a number of Reform rabbis have taken the stand that only the parents—not religious authorities and not the state—should have the right to decide whether a pregnancy should be allowed to continue or else be aborted, and therefore, that all laws restricting abortion should be abolished. This minority view represents the most radical position of any religious group on the subject of legalizing abortion.

THE PROTESTANT VIEWPOINT

The Protestant position on abortion is based on an age-old concept of protecting the sanctity of "life." Although Protestant theology does not concern itself with the intricacies of "animation" and "ensoulment," Protestantism regards abortion as the killing of a life already conceived and permits it only for the most serious reasons, and certainly not for the mere convenience of the mother.

The only interdenominational document ever issued on abortion by Protestants in the United States (at this writing) is a policy statement made by the General Board of the National Council of Churches of Christ on February 23, 1961. This statement approved hospital abortion only "when the health or life of the mother is at stake." At the same time, abortion as a birth control method was condemned and the "protection of the sanctity of life" was stressed.

In the past decade a number of Protestant denominations have declared their own positions on abortion. One of the most stringent statements was issued at the Lambeth Conference in 1958, in which Anglican Bishops and the American Episcopalian representative concurred that "Christians reject the practice of induced abortion . . . save at the dictate of strict and undeniable medical necessity. The plight of families, or indeed of governments, trapped in hopeless poverty and overpopulation, may well help us understand why they think abortion more merciful than the slow starvation which looms ahead. Still, the sacredness of life is, in Christian eyes, an absolute which should not be violated."

A similar viewpoint was recorded at the 174th General Assembly of The United Presbyterian Church in the U.S.A. in May 1962. Condemning induced abortion as a means of family planning, this document stated: "The fetus is a human life to be protected by the criminal law from the moment when the ovum is fertilized. The sanctity of the mother's life and that of the child should be respected and preserved." The question of which life should have priority in being saved—the mother's or the child's—"must be decided on the basis of the specific medical problems involved."

More lenient than the Lambeth and Presbyterian documents was a paper released by the executive committee of the Church Council of the American Lutheran Church following its meetings, January 7–9, 1963, which stated: "In our judgment therapeutic abortion is permitted when: a) the life of the mother is involved; b) where the mother's health is threatened with severe physical or mental impairment; c) but not in cases of possible deformity."

The churches of the American Baptist Convention will review in 1968 a request to "support legislation in their states to make abortion legal in cases of rape, incest, mental incompetence, or where there is danger to the health of the mother." Local churches were previously asked to make a "thorough study" of the abortion issue. Ministerial groups were to be guided by authorities in the fields of medicine, sociology, and theology—and "findings of local churches, ministerial groups, and other study groups be forwarded to the 1968 Resolutions Committee for their use in formulating a more definitive statement on this subject."

The 1968 General Convention of the American Lutheran Church will receive a draft of a proposed statement from its Commission on Research and Social Action. The proposal urges that laws governing therapeutic abortion should be amended to permit one not only when the mother's life is endangered but also when her physical or mental health is threatened, and in instances of incest, forcible rape, and when the mother is barely more than a child herself. In addition, substantial risk that the infant might be born with grave mental or physical defects would also permit consideration of a therapeutic abortion.

Some more "radical" Protestants—at the 1963 General Assembly of the Unitarian-Universalists—were in support of legalizing abortion for the above reasons, but in addition, for "some compelling reason, physical, psychological, mental, spiritual, or economic." This would practically result in abortion on request when approved by a group of medical and possibly lay authorities.

On the other hand, several eminent contemporary Protestant theologians, such as Karl Barth and Dietrich Bonhoeffer, have emphatically stated that they believed abortion is immoral.

In summary, the Protestant viewpoint on abortion resembles more than it differs from the Catholic viewpoint. However, many Protestant groups are increasingly supporting legal reform of existing abortion laws, while the Catholic Church at present is categorically opposed to any such changes.

11

Abortion Laws in Foreign Countries

For thousands of years women in almost every society have resorted to abortion as a means of preventing birth. Today, according to demographer Ronald Freedman, *abortion is the most widely used single method of birth control throughout the world*. Once granted the desperate need for worldwide control of population, it follows that where contraceptive efforts or methods have failed, recourse must be had to safe, medically performed, legalized abortion, when sought by the single or married woman.

Legalized abortion, when properly performed, carries a risk of complications or death which is only about one sixth of the risk created by an uninterrupted pregnancy and childbirth. On the other hand, criminal abortion is the largest single cause of maternal death in those countries which make it a crime to perform an abortion except to save the woman's life. Maternal mortality from criminal abortion throughout the world constitutes one of the most tragic public health problems today.

Depending upon a number of historical, ethical, cultural, religious, and population density factors, many countries now have laws approving abortion under different sets of medical and social circumstances.

JAPAN

Soon after the close of World War II Japan was faced with an acute population problem that became a national emergency. In 1948 the Japanese Diet (parliament) passed the Eugenic Protection Law, broadened in the next few years to provide legalized abortion on demand for reasons of health or economics. The cost of an abortion has been $10 or less, and to the worker who has industrial or government health insurance or to the very poor, abortion is free. As a result of legalized abortion, Japan has succeeded in cutting the formerly high birth rate approximately in half.

SOVIET UNION, BULGARIA, HUNGARY

The Russians, while not so hard pressed to stem their population, nevertheless were intent on increasing female as well as male productivity, and hence, postponing motherhood. In 1955 a law was passed legalizing abortion on demand—mainly to help the average Russian family achieve a higher standard of living by limiting family size. Such legalization was also initiated to eliminate criminal abortion and its hazards.

Abortion is permitted upon the request of a woman and proper authorization of a physician, providing there are no medical contraindications to it. Termination of pregnancy is allowed only in hospitals or comparable medical institutions. The cost is about $1.

In 1956 Bulgaria and Hungary followed the Soviet lead in legalizing abortion on demand for basically the same reasons. However, only after consideration of all the medical and social factors is an abortion approved. In cases of medical necessity, as decided by a committee of three physicians, no fee is charged for the procedure. For interruptions of pregnancy for nonmedical reasons, there is a nominal charge.

POLAND, CZECHOSLOVAKIA, YUGOSLAVIA

In 1954 Poland passed a law legalizing abortion for medical reasons alone, but because of the tremendous numbers of women admitted to hospitals suffering from the results of criminally performed abortions, the grounds for abortion were liberalized in 1956 to include economic and psychological hardship, medically certified. If the husband or wife is covered by health insurance, abortion is free; otherwise, the fee is less than $10 in state hospitals. Private doctors charge about $40.

Czechoslovakia started in 1957 to authorize abortions in very specified medical conditions, as well as in certain limited social situations—advanced age, numerous children, loss or disability of spouse, broken home, the woman's predominant responsibility for supporting the family, social problems of an unmarried woman, and pregnancy due to rape or another criminal act.

In 1961 the laws were further liberalized to include such reasons for abortion as the existence of three children or more, and as risk to the standard of living where the woman is the breadwinner of the family. The cost of abortion, which had been generally nominal, was waived altogether.

In 1962, owing to the Czech government's concern about the declining birth rate, abortion laws were tightened. Applications had to be filed in the woman's home district and, if approved by a commission, the operation had to be performed in that district. Nominal fees were reinstituted, except in cases of medical necessity.

Yugoslavia enacted its present abortion law in 1960. It authorized interruption of pregnancy when the life or health of the mother is threatened, when there is a high likelihood that the infant would be born with serious physical or mental defects, when pregnancy is the result of a criminal act, and when pregnancy would result in difficult and insoluble personal, family, or material conditions. A commission consisting of two physicians and a social worker must approve all applications for abortion, which is performed in approved medical institutions.

RUMANIA

Rumania, which had a liberal abortion law, enacted in 1966 an unpopular restricting law in an effort to boost the birth rate. This is another example of how abortion legislation reflects governmental planning of population trends.

In the exceptional cases in which abortion is currently allowed, the cost is about $2.50, but the strictness of the new law has resulted in skyrocketing costs of illegal abortions, often done by medical students.

ICELAND, SWEDEN, DENMARK, NORWAY, FINLAND

While not as liberal as Japan, the Soviet Union, and the majority of the eastern European countries, all the Scandinavian countries have laws legalizing abortion, beginning with Iceland in the 1930's. To 1) the medical indications for abortion regarding threats to the mother's health and mental well-being, 2) the possibility of her bearing an abnormal child, and 3) pregnancies resulting from rape or incest, is added consideration of all related social circumstances. Abortion is sometimes performed in situations in which the conditions of life and environmental circumstances of the mother are such that having a baby might gravely affect her physical or mental health.

Scandinavian laws have taken into account the now-accepted premise that social factors are inseparable from an individual's physical and mental health, and therefore, must be included in consideration of therapeutic abortion. Authorization is given by two or more physicians or a special board or committee, and the procedure must be done only in approved medical institutions. The cost averages $75 for surgery and hospitalization.

BRITAIN

In Britain, where abortion had been legal only in order to save the life of the woman, several judicial interpretations had allowed pregnancy to be interrupted if it endangered the woman's physical or mental health. Despite a governmental report of 1939 urging clarification and liberalization of existing national laws, it was not until 1967 that both Houses of Parliament gave final approval to a bill broadening the indications for legal abortion.

This 1967 law included as reasons endangerment of the mother's physical or mental health, threat to the health of any existing children, and substantial risk of the birth of a severely handicapped child.

COUNTRIES AUTHORIZING ABORTION FOR MEDICAL REASONS

Abortion is authorized in a number of countries, not only to save the mother's life, but also to preserve her health.

In Switzerland the abortion laws, while providing criminal penalties for abortion induced by the woman herself or by someone else, allow interruption of pregnancy by a licensed doctor in a situation when risk to the mother's life cannot otherwise be averted—or when pregnancy presents a serious threat to the woman's health in a grave and permanent way. In such a situation, the physician who is to perform the abortion must have the written consent of the woman and the concurrence of a second physician.

West Germany and East Germany both had had much more liberal abortion laws in the immediate post–World War II period. But since the 1950's, efforts made to reduce the number of abortions resulted in authorization only for medical and eugenic reasons.

Tunisian law permits abortion when the woman's health is

threatened by pregnancy or when the parents have at least five living children.

Honduras, Peru, Mexico, and Syria all have laws restricting abortion to those instances in which continuing a pregnancy endangers the woman's health.

COUNTRIES AUTHORIZING ABORTION ONLY TO SAVE THE WOMAN'S LIFE

According to a decree of 1955, abortion is illegal in France—unless the "life of the mother is gravely threatened" and this fact is attested to and certified by three physicians who further must state that the danger to the mother's life cannot be averted in any other way. It has been estimated that in France two thousand illegal abortions are carried out for every single abortion that is legally performed. The number of *illegal* abortions is equal to the number of live births in that country. At a time when tuberculosis in the Western world has been progressively decreasing, one-half of the French authorized abortions have been done because of pulmonary tuberculosis in the mother.

Among other countries in which abortion may be performed only to save the mother's life are Venezuela, Chile, Turkey, and Western Australia.

Throughout the world, especially where abortion laws are stringent, women have attempted to abort themselves. In Latin America, which has the fastest growing birth rate of any area of the world, the leading cause of *death* among women between the ages of fifteen and forty-five is reported to be a crude and unsterile method of self-abortion called "la sonda," the probe. It is referred to by physicians as "el carnicero"—the butcher.

La sonda is any pointed metal instrument about twelve inches in length that is used to rupture the placenta, causing uterine contractions and eventual expulsion of the fetus. Most of the women who use la sonda are married and are mothers already. It is estimated that such an instrument, which can be merely a knitting needle or a car aerial broken in half, is employed several million times a year throughout the Latin American countries.

According to a *New York Times* article of September 17, 1967, for many women the use of la sonda results in "massive hemorrhages, tenacious infections, and painful deaths."

12

Abortion Laws in the United States

The majority of current American abortion laws are similar to those of such countries as Turkey, Iraq, Afghanistan, Sudan, Portugal, and France—authorizing abortion only for rigidly specified medical reasons.

With certain exceptions the laws in forty-five American states permit abortion only "if necessary to preserve the life of the mother." In spite of such strict legal medical requirements, most of these states quite inconsistently do not even require such a lifesaving procedure to be performed by a physician.

THE HISTORY OF AMERICAN ABORTION LAWS

The beginnings of American abortion laws date back to thirteenth-century England, when Church dogma was integrated into the English common law. Abortion, previously considered in England only an ecclesiastical offense, then became a civil offense in cases of an already formed and "animated" fetus. Quickening—that time during gestation when the mother first feels fetal movements in her uterus—soon replaced the animation theory in this law.

According to Lawrence Lader's *Abortion*, a definitive book on the subject, there is little evidence that abortion was prosecuted under common law after England's break with the Church. However, in 1803 the first British legislation on abortion, known as the Ellenborough Act, replaced the seldom-enforced common law with more stringent penalties for abortion, both before and after quickening. The Ellenborough Act, rather incidentally, included abortion by poisoning (no other abortion techniques were mentioned), along with dozens of other crimes ranging from poisoning in general to robbery, stabbing, and murder.

These English abortion laws served as models for the early American abortion laws, a number of states continuing to keep the ruling regarding quickening in their subsequent legislation as late as the early 1900's. Between 1828 and 1835 New York, Ohio, Indiana, and Missouri legalized abortion in cases of medical necessity, a provision that nearly all the other states eventually added to their laws. However, from 1821 up until 1956, many states have periodically *increased* their restrictions on abortion.

THE UNFORTUNATE RESULTS OF CURRENT LAWS

In spite of rigid enforcement of these nineteenth-century laws, abortion in this country in the twentieth century has become an enormous public health problem. With the passing of every hour, an estimated 125 women are willingly risking their lives at the hands of illegal abortionists in order to terminate an unwanted pregnancy. Any public health problem that seriously affects 3,000 women every day—1,000,000 every year (and the majority of these are married)—obviously indicates the need for changing the current practices.

PROPOSED CHANGES IN ABORTION LAWS

A group of distinguished American attorneys, who constitute the American Law Institute, proposed in 1962 a Model Penal Code as a means of effecting basic changes in the abortion laws of every state. According to the Model Penal Code, Section 230.3:

> A licensed physician is justified in terminating a pregnancy if he believes there is substantial risk that continuance of the pregnancy would gravely impair the physical or mental health of the mother or that the child would be born with grave physical or mental defect, or that the pregnancy resulted from rape, incest or other felonious intercourse. All illicit intercourse with a girl below the age of 16 shall be deemed felonious for purposes of this subsection (2). Justifiable abortions shall be performed only in a licensed hospital except in case of emergency when hospital facilities are unavailable.

In 1967 Colorado and North Carolina passed new abortion legislation patterned on the Model Penal Code. North Carolina, however, requires a four-month residency. California also approved similar changes in its abortion laws in 1967, but it does not permit abortion where the fetus may be physically or mentally impaired. In the early part of 1968 Georgia and Maryland passed abortion reform bills. Georgia's new statute requires that the woman and her physician swear that she is a resident; there is, however, no residency requirement in the Maryland law. Mississippi passed a new law in 1966 that not only permits abortion in case of danger to the mother's life but also when the pregnancy resulted from rape.

Abortion bills were introduced in 1967 in the following states but failed to pass the legislatures or were vetoed: Alabama, Arizona, Connecticut, Florida, Georgia, Hawaii, Illinois, Indiana, Iowa, Maine, Maryland, Michigan, Minnesota, Mississippi, Missouri, Nebraska, Nevada, New Mexico,

New York, Ohio, Oklahoma, Oregon, Pennsylvania, Rhode Island, Texas, and Wisconsin.

Fifteen of these states were considering changes along the lines of the Model Penal Code. The others were considering changes much less liberal.

There were twenty-one states in which no bill was introduced in 1967: Alaska, Arkansas, Delaware, Idaho, Kansas, Kentucky, Louisiana, Massachusetts, Montana, New Hampshire, New Jersey, North Dakota, South Carolina, South Dakota, Tennessee, Utah, Vermont, Virginia, Washington, West Virginia, and Wyoming.

In the July 11, 1967 issue of *Look*, senior editor Jack Starr wrote of various reactions of Colorado religious, medical, and legal authorities after Colorado became the first American state to liberalize its abortion laws. According to Mr. Starr, one of those who welcomed the new law was District Attorney Floyd Marks of Adams County, who related the following story to Mr. Starr as an example of the kind of personal tragedy that could have been averted by an authorized abortion:

" . . . a 14-year-old mentally retarded girl . . . was impregnated by her father. A public hospital in Denver was unable to perform an abortion, and she had to have her baby. What happened? The father is in prison. The family is on relief. The girl is under a psychiatrist's care. God knows where the baby is."

The first advance in changing the nineteenth-century abortion laws in an English-speaking country was made in 1938 by an eminent British surgeon, Alec Bourne. The first English Abortion Statute enacted in 1803 made all abortions illegal, with no exception for therapeutic abortion. Dr. Bourne made a public announcement that he proposed to perform an abortion on a fourteen-year-old girl who had been impregnated through rape by several soldiers. He was promptly arrested after completing the procedure and charged with commission of a felony, in which a verdict of "guilty" could result in life imprisonment.

This famous case, *Bourne v. the Crown*, was labeled by the London *Daily Express* "one of the most important in medical history," for not only did it open an "unspeakable" subject that had been closed for a century, but it forced the courts to define the guidelines for medical abortion. The judge, sympathetic to the defendant, summed up in his instructions to the jury the discussions concerning the meaning of the phrase, "preserving the life of the mother," and closely equated "life" and "health." In addition to the judge's statement that "life depends on health," he declared that anyone who for religious reasons believes an abortion is never justifiable "ought not to be a doctor practicing in that branch of medicine, for, if a case arose where the life of a woman could be saved by performing the operation and the doctor refused to permit it because of some religious opinion, he would be in grave peril of being brought before this court on a charge of manslaughter by negligence."

The judge further stated that a physician could interrupt a pregnancy if he thought that allowing it to continue would "make the woman a physical or mental wreck." This was the first statement ever made in legal circles regarding a justification for abortion if pregnancy were a threat to a woman's emotional health. The jury acquitted Dr. Bourne.

The efforts initiated by doctors and jurists, and by attorneys of the American Law Institute to liberalize abortion laws are beginning to show results. How long it will take before all fifty states change their abortion laws remains one of the unanswerable medical-legal questions of the near future, but abortion is certainly on the way to shedding its old status as a criminal act and becoming a medical decision and a hospital experience.

13

Therapeutic Abortion

Therapeutic abortion is the term applied to a legal abortion performed in a hospital by a qualified physician, almost always for medical or psychiatric reasons. It is the intentional emptying of a pregnant uterus, usually within the first three months of pregnancy, when the fetus is still insufficiently developed to be able to survive outside the womb. While in most states therapeutic abortion is allowed to be performed only to preserve the life of the mother, a few states permit consideration of the mother's physical or mental health as sufficient reasons for therapeutic interruption of pregnancy.

In the United States today increased medical knowledge and improved prenatal care have led to the earlier recognition and effective treatment of a variety of illnesses which, only a generation ago, would have been fatal to the mother if pregnancy were allowed to continue. Therefore, interruption of pregnancy to save the mother's life is seldom required—even for severe heart, lung, liver, or kidney disease, any of which had in decades past been a common indication for therapeutic abortion. The majority of therapeutic abortions are done today either for psychiatric reasons or because of the likelihood of a deformed infant resulting from rubella in the mother during the first three months of pregnancy.

With the exception of Catholic hospitals, where therapeutic abortions are absolutely prohibited, it is apparent that the majority of the therapeutic operations performed in American hospitals for medical reasons are "therapeutic" medically but are technically illegal. While therapeutic abortion practices vary widely from hospital to hospital and from physician to physician, only 8,000 induced abortions are "legal" out of the estimated 1,000,000 abortions performed each year in this country.

CURRENT MEDICAL TECHNIQUES

"D and C," which stands for dilatation (of the cervix) and curettage (scraping of the lining of the uterus) is the standard method used to perform a therapeutic abortion before the thirteenth week of pregnancy. It may be done under pentothal, ether, gas, or even under a local anesthetic. The cervix is dilated or stretched in order to permit entrance into the uterus of a curette, a long, thin metal instrument with a scraping loop at its end. A D and C usually takes about thirty minutes to do, and requires about a day or two in the hospital. Complications and aftereffects are extremely rare and there is little evidence that subsequent fertility is affected.

If an abortion must be performed *after* the thirteenth week of pregnancy, the choice of procedures usually rests between a hysterotomy and a newer technique using injected hypertonic glucose or salt solution. A hysterotomy is a small-scale caesarean section in which an incision is made in the lower abdomen and in the uterus itself, and the products of conception removed. In the injection technique a small needle, like those used for spinal taps, is inserted either through the vagina or the abdomen, and amniotic fluid (the fluid that surrounds the embryo) is removed by means of a syringe. This amniotic fluid is then replaced with an equal or slightly larger volume of fifty percent glucose solution or twenty percent saline solution, causing the fetus to be expelled from the uterus usually eighteen to forty-eight hours after the injection.

In recent years the Russians have developed a still newer technique of performing abortion by means of a device that dilates the cervix by electro-vibration and empties the uterus by negative-pressure vacuum. This "vacuum" method takes less than two minutes to perform before the twelfth week of pregnancy, and is reportedly gentler than a D and C and carries a minimal risk of injury and blood loss. This method has been adapted and is being used successfully in the United States.

In cases of ectopic or extrauterine pregnancy, when the fertilized ovum implants itself not in the lining of the uterus but in some abnormal site (usually in a fallopian tube—less commonly in the abdominal cavity, an ovary, or the cervix), surgery is required to save the mother's life and should be performed immediately upon diagnosis. Probably because no fetus can survive outside of the uterus and because of the mortal danger it presents to the mother, operation for removal of ectopic pregnancy is not classified as a therapeutic "abortion."

For practical purposes, there have yet to be discovered any safe or reliable *nonsurgical* means of inducing abortion. Methotrexate or aminopterin, a drug used in treating leukemia and certain forms of cancer, often causes abortion. However, if it should fail, the baby is very likely to be born with gross and multiple congenital abnormalities. X-ray treatment to the pelvic area also usually results in fetal death and subsequent abortion, but again, should it fail, the infant will almost certainly be grossly deformed at birth.

THE DANGERS OF "DO-IT-YOURSELF" ABORTION

While figures on the number of annual deaths from illegal or self-induced abortions are hard to come by, it is estimated that between 500 and 1,000 women die from this cause each year in the United States. In addition to these needless deaths, thousands of other women suffer grave and agonizing illnesses as a result of attempts at self-abortion.

No woman would think of removing her own appendix, yet many women have in their ignorance attempted what only a skilled surgeon can safely accomplish. Some women, knowing the dangers involved, hope that by initiating vaginal bleeding they can then be "legally" admitted to a hospital for proper completion of an "incomplete" abortion.

Women, in desperation, have resorted to vaginal douches of such toxic substances as lysol, potassium permanganate, detergents, and hydrogen peroxide. They have inserted into the uterus such objects as wires, knitting needles, coat hangers, paintbrushes, rubber tubes, chopsticks, and cotton swabs. These attempts at abortion have resulted in severe infections, massive hemorrhages, pelvic peritonitis, tetanus, gas gangrene, pulmonary embolism, thrombophlebitis, kidney damage, rupture of the uterus—not to mention permanent sterility.

THE FUTURE OF ABORTION

For the thousands of years that women have resorted to abortion, men have opposed it on ethical grounds for much of that span of time. It is only now, in the second half of the twentieth century, that men in all parts of the world are beginning to agree with women that abortion has its place in society as a backstop against birth control "accidents." The realistic recognize that no matter how successful science may be in perfecting more effective methods of birth prevention, abortion will still be the answer in eliminating the unwanted pregnancies that result from contraceptive failures.

In a famous speech presented in May 1966, Garrett Hardin, Ph.D., Professor of Biology at the University of California, Santa Barbara, stated: "Experience indicates that unwanted pregnancies occur most often among the underaged, the overaged, and the psychologically disturbed. The underaged become pregnant because they cross the sexual threshold before they think they are going to, and do so unprepared. The overaged, entering the menopause, neglect contraceptive precautions because they *think* they are sterile. The psychologically disturbed, typically a neurotic woman involved in a marriage that is going on the rocks, behave impulsively and sometimes with destructive intent. None of these three types of women is a good bet for motherhood at the time when contraceptive failure occurs."*

The growing awareness of the high degree of safety of legalized, professionally performed abortions may also be contributing to the new acceptance of abortion. In those countries where abortion is readily available, the mortality rate of legal abortion is "exceedingly low," according to Dr. Christopher Tietze of New York, who is associate director of the biomedical division of the Population Council. At a recent international conference on "Fertility and Family Planning: A World View," held at the University of Michigan, Ann Arbor, Dr. Tietze presented statistics on abortion deaths in Japan and eastern Europe. In Japan, where legal abortions rose from 2,994,000 in 1950–53 to 5,138,000 in 1959–63, the death rate per 100,000 abortions dropped from 8.5 (253 deaths) in 1950–53, to 4.1 (210 deaths) in 1959–63.

In Hungary, where there were 21 deaths for the 670,000 legal abortions in 1960–63, the death rate was 3.1 per 100,000, he said. In Czechoslovakia, the rate was 6.8 for 1957–60, but it dropped to 1.2 for 1961–64. In Yugoslavia, eight deaths occurred in 1960–61 among 177,000 legal abortions, a rate of 4.5 per 100,000.

Perhaps the most realistic attitude has been that of the Rev. Robert F. Drinan, a Roman Catholic priest and dean of the Boston College Law School, favoring *repeal* of American abortion laws. He expressed this view before an international

---

* In 1968 Dr. Hardin further suggested that the wrong question has been posed. "How can we justify an abortion?" should be replaced by the proper question in today's world: "How can we justify *compulsory pregnancy?*"

abortion conference in the fall of 1967 sponsored by the Harvard Divinity School and the Kennedy Foundation. The January 8, 1968, *New York Times* quoted Father Drinan as saying that the model abortion law "won't reach the real problem, namely that 80 to 85 percent of the abortions are for married women who just don't want this third, fourth, or fifth child." He felt abortion is a social problem and not a medical problem, and in conclusion, he stated: "If you say a problem exists, and that women will get an abortion and the law can't prevent this, all right then, withdraw the law. If we're going to have to change, I say the nonlaw has greater potential for solving the problem than the Model Penal Code."

Both Dr. Garrett Hardin and Father Drinan made references to medications currently being tested that could be taken the "morning after" to inhibit implantation of the fertilized egg, or taken on the twenty-sixth or last day of the menstrual cycle to induce a menstrual flow before the woman would know whether or not she was pregnant. Then drug-induced abortion would have no more emotional impact on the woman than having a regular menstrual period. After all, women spontaneously abort more than one-third of their embryos without being aware of it.

Such an abortion pill could virtually prevent the need for surgical means of abortion and automatically mollify religious attitudes and legal prohibitions. To quote Dr. Hardin, as he concluded his lecture:

"It is difficult to see that society has any interest in controlling the distribution of harmless abortifacients when they become available. Indeed, society has an interest in making them readily available to all, for only by giving women complete and sure control of births can we bring to a successful conclusion the emancipation of women begun more than a century ago."

PART III

THE PREGNANT WOMAN

14

Tests for Pregnancy

Since the days of ancient Egypt, when the urine of a pregnant woman was known to induce the flowering of plants, many tests for diagnosing pregnancy have been based on demonstrating the presence of increased amounts of one particular hormone in the body fluids, especially in the urine. This hormone, called human chorionic gonadotrophin (HCG), is produced in early pregnancy in very large quantities by the placenta, the structure which is attached to the uterine wall and nourishes the embryo. Upon delivery, the placenta is referred to as the afterbirth.

Therefore, the placenta functions like a temporary endocrine gland, producing HCG within a few days of the implantation of the fertilized ovum. As the placenta develops and becomes an organ in itself, it also produces estrogen and progesterone until near the end of pregnancy. The formation of HCG, which is usually detectable in pregnancy tests within two or three weeks of implantation, decreases as the pregnancy progresses.

The chorion in the term, human chorionic gonadotrophin, refers to the outer of the two membranes forming the sac that encloses the fetus in the uterus. The term, gonadotrophin, refers to the sex gland-stimulating effect of the hormone.

PREGNANCY TESTS USING ANIMALS

The most commonly used pregnancy tests in the past four decades have relied upon the reaction of animal sex organs to the injection of small quantities of urine from the woman being tested. Of the great number of such tests that have been proposed through the years using different animal species, the following have been the most widely used:

THE ASCHHEIM–ZONDEK TEST

The "A–Z" test, introduced in 1927, was the first valid pregnancy test and the first to use animals. The urine is injected under the skin of five immature female white mice, and reinjected five times in the next two days. Nearly 100 hours after the first injection the mice are killed and their ovaries examined. Hemorrhagic changes in the mouse ovaries indicate the presence of HCG in the test urine, and the reaction is then reported as positive for pregnancy.

THE FRIEDMAN TEST

Introduced in 1930, this is an equally reliable yet simpler variation of the A–Z test. A mature, isolated female rabbit is used, the urine specimen being injected into an ear vein. Within forty-eight hours, the rabbit's ovaries are examined for signs that the rabbit has ovulated, indicating the presence of increased HCG in the urine specimen. The Friedman test may also be done using blood serum instead of urine.

THE KUPPERMAN TEST

In this test the urine is injected into the abdominal cavity of a female rat. After two hours the ovaries are examined. Marked redness due to increased blood circulation is the laboratory sign that points to a positive diagnosis of pregnancy.

THE HOGBEN TEST

The test animal is the female South African clawed toad, *Xenopus laevis*. The urine is injected into the toad's dorsal lymph sac and, within twenty-four hours, if the reaction is positive, the animal extrudes large numbers of eggs. The same animal can be used repeatedly for this test.

THE GALLI-MAININI TEST

The ordinary male frog is used for this test, in which the urine is also injected into the dorsal lymph sac. Presence of HCG in the woman's urine will cause ejection of sperm from the frog's testes, and sperm will be present in the frog's urine within two to four hours of the injection. The same animal can be used repeatedly as in the Hogben test.

The accuracy of all these tests is better than ninety-five percent. If a woman is pregnant, there is less than a five percent chance that the test will be "false negative." Similarly, if she is not pregnant, there is less than a five percent chance that the test will be "false positive."

To help decrease the possibility of errors with any of the tests just described, women are advised to: 1) drink nothing after seven P.M. of the day before the test and void before retiring; 2) collect the first morning voiding in a clean, dry container and then pour three or four ounces into a clean, dry stoppered bottle; and 3) keep the specimen in the refrigerator if more than an hour will elapse between the passage of the urine and the actual start of the pregnancy test.

NEWER METHODS OF PREGNANCY TESTING

A test tube method of diagnosing pregnancy was first sought as long ago as 1903. However, it was not until 1960 that such a test, which has the great convenience of not requiring animal colonies, was developed using either urine or blood.

There are now several variations of the initial method, but they all are based on *immunological* techniques—not unlike those forming the basis for blood typing or blood tests for syphilis. These immunological tests take anywhere from two minutes to two hours to give the diagnosis and are 94–99 percent reliable when used ten days or more after the first missed period. Because of their accuracy and ease of performance, the immunological tests for pregnancy have replaced the animal pregnancy tests, except in special situations.

For the past several years there has successfully been used a method which is both a test for pregnancy *and* a treatment for the woman whose period is otherwise delayed beyond the expected date. Its main application is during the first two to ten days after a missed period when there is not yet a sufficient amount of HCG to give reliable results in any of the other pregnancy tests.

In this test the physician usually prescribes two or three days of estrogen and progesterone combined in one tablet. Within one week after the last dose, about ninety percent of women who are not pregnant will begin menstruation. If a woman is pregnant, no bleeding will occur. There has been no evidence that the tablet contributes to abortion or in any way adversely affects the fetus or the pregnancy. Furthermore, it does not interfere with any of the other methods of pregnancy diagnosis.

15

Safer Pregnancy

One index of the general "healthiness" of any country's population is its statistics on maternal mortality—the risk which a woman takes to bring forth a child. In the United States, maternal mortality has dropped from around 60 per 10,000 live births in 1915 to less than 4 per 10,000 live births in the 1960's.

This dramatic decline in the mother's risk of death is due in great part to better and more universally applied prenatal health care. This in itself leads to earlier recognition and, therefore, prompter and more effective treatment—and often prevention—of the most serious threats to the woman's health: infection, hemorrhage, and toxemia of pregnancy (a disorder peculiar to the pregnant woman, accompanied by severe water retention, high blood pressure, and abnormal amounts of proteins in the urine). Most infections yield to today's markedly superior antibiotic and chemotherapeutic drugs; severe loss of blood can now be treated by immediate, and if necessary, repeated transfusions made possible by the greater availability of blood; toxemia is better controlled by new diuretic and blood pressure-lowering medications.

The other significant factor in the declining maternal mortality rate has been a continuing trend toward virtually 100 percent hospital deliveries, as opposed to home deliveries and deliveries in transit. In addition, newer chemical and electronic diagnostic tests enable earlier and more precise recognition of potential hazards for mother and child during pregnancy and labor. In fact, an increasing number of medical centers are beginning to set up intensive care units on the labor floors specifically designed for the moment-to-moment monitoring and rapid treatment of the mother with special obstetrical problems.

DIAGNOSTIC TESTS

Many of the newer diagnostic tests are especially concerned with the development and location of the placenta, in addition to early discovery of multiple pregnancy, abnormal conditions in the mother and child, and the birth position of the baby. The placenta, besides its glandular functions in secreting essential hormones, is actually an intricate network of blood vessels allowing the mother's blood vessels and those of the unborn baby to mingle closely. The mother's blood does not flow through the baby's blood vessels. However, nourishing food substances and oxygen in the mother's blood, filtered through the blood vessel walls into the baby's blood, circulate throughout the baby's bloodstream. Waste materials are carried by the baby's bloodstream to the placenta where they are filtered out through the vessel walls into the mother's blood and later excreted by her.

An abnormally placed placenta is one of the causes of serious bleeding in the last three months of pregnancy. In recent years placentography has been developed for accurately locating the position of the placenta. One method uses a harmless radioactive iodine compound which is injected into an arm vein of the mother. The radioactivity is picked up by the placenta and can be measured by an external detector placed in different positions on the mother's abdomen.

A promising recent diagnostic technique uses ultrasound waves and their "echoes" (sonar)—in the same manner as radar uses radio waves—to determine more exactly the location of the placenta, to detect multiple pregnancies, to look for abnormal conditions and abnormal fetal positions such as breech, and to quite precisely measure the size of the fetal head where a narrow birth passage is suspected. Ultrasound equipment can be used painlessly without harm to the fetus or the mother, and can sometimes detect the fetal heartbeat as early as six weeks after conception.

Advances in technology have also led to the discovery that the fetal heart can inscribe its own electrocardiogram from as early as the twelfth week of gestation. The fetal electrocardiogram, recorded from electrodes placed on the mother's abdomen, can be used to confirm the presence of a live fetus in situations where routine pregnancy tests may be inconclusive, long before the mother can feel "life" or the physician can hear the fetal heartbeat. At a later stage it can establish the early diagnosis of multiple pregnancy. Used during labor, the fetal electrocardiogram can detect such difficulties as problems of fetal circulation from the placenta or from pressure on the umbilical cord. It may also indicate that there is undue pressure on the baby's head.

Recording and monitoring of intrauterine pressure during labor was begun ten years ago for the study of uterine contractions in spontaneous labor, false labor, and after medications given to induce or stimulate labor. The intrauterine pressure tracing from a pressure sensor inserted in the uterine cavity also provides a guide to the safe injection of hypertonic saline into the amniotic cavity when labor must be induced in midterm.

TREATMENT OF ILLNESSES DURING PREGNANCY

The greatest cause of maternal mortality in the United States not resulting directly from pregnancy and childbirth has been heart disease, which affects approximately two percent of pregnant women. Fully ninety percent of this two percent suffer from rheumatic heart disease, a result of one or more attacks of rheumatic fever, which inflames and scars the heart valves; the remaining ten percent is comprised chiefly of those women having congenital heart defects, in which the heart or a major blood vessel near the heart fails to develop normally during the period of fetal maturation. A small minority of women have such conditions as hypertensive heart disease, coronary heart disease, kyphoscoliotic heart disease, and other rare forms of myocarditis.

Pregnancy, even more than delivery, places an increased burden on the heart and on the circulation. The woman whose heart function has already been restricted by underlying heart disease may find that her heart cannot keep up with the demands imposed on it by the pregnant state. In advanced cases of heart disease when the risk of continuing the pregnancy is grave, therapeutic abortion is indicated. In earlier years, therapeutic abortion had been carried out almost routinely even in moderately severe cases. The great majority of such cases today are carried safely through term and delivery by means of close supervision, fluid and salt restriction, diuretics, and often digitalis.

Fortunately, the incidence of rheumatic fever has declined markedly in the last twenty years for many reasons, among them prompt and effective antibiotic treatment of streptococcal infections which are the forerunners of rheumatic fever. Great progress in heart surgery has been responsible for the decline in the numbers of women of childbearing age suffering from congenital heart defects, as most such defects have already been corrected in infancy and childhood. In addition, closed heart and open heart surgery has safely been performed on women with rheumatic and congenital heart disease when necessary *even during pregnancy*, with very little added risk to the mother or the fetus.

Although *diabetes mellitus* was described more than two thousand years ago in the Ebers Papyrus of ancient Egypt, there was no effective treatment for the "disease of thirst" until the discovery of insulin in 1921 by Frederick G. Banting, a young Canadian surgeon, and Charles H. Best, a graduate student in physiology. Before this history-making event, pregnant diabetics were few in number; only one out of every twenty diabetic women in their reproductive years was able to become pregnant and most of these pregnancies ended in therapeutic or spontaneous abortion or stillbirth—the chance that a pregnancy in a diabetic mother could result in a living child was less than fifty percent.

In the more than forty years since the advent of insulin therapy, an increasing number of young diabetics have been able to reach childbearing age and have been able to conceive at a rate approaching that of non-diabetics. In the same period of time, the fetal survival rate has improved dramatically—to over eighty percent. Recent methods of treating pregnant diabetics have advanced to such a degree that, where adequate medical and hospital facilities are available, even a woman with severe diabetes stands a seventy-five percent chance of successfully completing a pregnancy.

Pregnancy presents a stress to a woman's metabolism and may thus bring to light a diabetic tendency not previously recognized. Therefore, diabetes is diligently searched for by the physician, even in the early weeks of pregnancy. Partly for this reason, the incidence of known and discovered diabetes in pregnancy has risen to about one in one hundred.

The improved outlook for infants of diabetic mothers, while due in part to closer observation of the mother, early recognition and prompt treatment of infections, acidosis, and toxemia, nevertheless is most directly related to interruption of pregnancy some three to five weeks before the expected date of delivery—either by induction of labor or caesarean section. This is done because the hazard of fetal death increases during the last few weeks of pregnancy in diabetics. In addition, immediate recognition and handling of the problems of the infant born to a diabetic mother have contributed greatly to its better chances of survival.

Tuberculosis, though less prevalent than it was in the

general population, still affects an estimated one percent of pregnant women in the United States. However, earlier recognition by routine chest X-ray as part of prenatal care, together with curative drugs developed and employed since 1950, have changed the medical attitude toward pregnancy and tuberculosis. In the first half of the twentieth century tuberculosis was considered a grave complication of pregnancy, since pregnancy had an adverse effect on the disease and there was a high maternal mortality rate. For this reason, therapeutic abortion was usually recommended and carried out early in pregnancy.

Today therapeutic abortion is almost never resorted to in cases of maternal tuberculosis. Women with arrested tuberculosis run little risk that pregnancy will reactivate their disease, but they should consult a physician before deciding to become pregnant. Once such a woman is pregnant, she will need to be carefully followed not only throughout the course of her pregnancy but for at least a year after delivery. Antituberculosis medications are often given two months before delivery to prevent any possible recurrence of tuberculosis during the stresses of late pregnancy, labor, and delivery.

Women with active tuberculosis are advised not to become pregnant until the tuberculosis has been arrested. However, when active tuberculosis is discovered (usually on X-ray examination) in a pregnant woman, she is given one or more antituberculosis drugs, such as isoniazid tablets, para-aminosalicylic acid tablets, and/or streptomycin injections. These medicines have revolutionized the care of the pregnant woman with tuberculosis and have enabled many women to be cared for without recourse to prolonged hospitalization or bed rest.

Urinary tract infections are among the commonest and most serious complications of pregnancy. They may be localized in the bladder (cystitis) or the upper urinary tract (pyelitis) and kidney (pyelonephritis). Once symptoms develop, these infections are vigorously and effectively treated with newer, safe chemotherapeutic drugs. Many women, though they have no symptoms, are discovered through urinalysis to have bacteria in their urine (bacteriuria) or pus in their urine (pyuria) and are promptly treated with the same drugs. The search for hidden urinary tract infections, as well as the treatment of evident infections, has done much to prevent ensuing kidney damage and related high blood pressure.

Since 1957 when it was found that influenza could produce much more serious complications in the pregnant woman, immunization with influenza vaccine has been strongly recommended for all expectant mothers. Similarly, the pregnant woman is especially susceptible to polio at any age, and therefore immunization with polio vaccine or administration of booster doses is strongly advised.

16

Control of Labor

Labor, one of nature's most awesome events, usually begins 280 days after conception in the average pregnancy. No one knows exactly what causes the onset of labor, but the dramatic process that follows unfolds in three stages. The first stage can be quite prolonged (from six to eighteen hours), during which time rhythmic uterine contractions start to propel the infant through the pelvis, while at the same time, the cervix becomes increasingly thinned out and dilated. The second stage of labor begins with full dilatation of the cervix and ends with the delivery of the baby. The third stage follows at this point and continues until the placenta and the fetal membranes have been delivered.

PELVIMETRY

The course of labor is greatly influenced by the anatomy of the mother's pelvis. Part of the physical examination of every pregnant woman is a pelvic examination in the usual manner, but with special attention to the bony structures. In addition, measurements are taken externally with a compasslike hand instrument called a pelvimeter.

If a difficult delivery is anticipated or a long labor shows little progress, *X-ray pelvimetry* is used for more accurate measurements of the size of the pelvis in comparison with the size of the baby's head, the largest and heaviest part of the baby. (Approximately ninety-five percent of all babies are born head first.)

THE SEARCH FOR PAINLESS CHILDBIRTH

As every woman is different and every pelvis is different, there is a great variation in the discomforts of labor and in the methods used to alleviate those discomforts. Safe relief of labor pain is one of the biggest challenges that confront the obstetrician. Because pain-relieving drugs filter through the placenta to the baby's blood and may depress the baby's respiratory center to the point that it is unable to breathe after birth, the doctor has to be cautious and selective in the type and amount of analgesic medication to be given. Furthermore, it must be given only at certain stages of labor to avoid slowing down the entire labor process. Intermittent inhalation anaesthesia is usually administered for the actual delivery.

Some women report they have experienced painless childbirth while under hypnosis. Preparation for hypnosis during labor usually begins before the seventh month of pregnancy, when posthypnotic suggestions are made to the effect that labor will be completely painless. Every two weeks the woman is given the same suggestions while in the hypnotic trance, and when labor begins, she is so indoctrinated that hypnotic sleep can be induced within a matter of seconds. Once under hypnosis, the woman is able to hear her doctor talk, can speak herself, and is able to have, without anaesthesia, a painless delivery, even when forceps are required. Certainly hypnosis is not suitable for all women but can be applied only in selected cases. It must be used only by qualified physicians who are experienced in such a procedure.

A large number of women in the past two decades have been trained for "natural childbirth." Although there are various methods, most employ the principle of counteracting the muscle tension of labor by relaxation of the muscles learned through a course of exercises practiced throughout pregnancy. The woman who is successful in learning her relaxation technique can, under normal circumstances, achieve a painless labor without drugs and, while fully conscious, watch her baby being born. The use of hypnotic suggestion undoubtedly plays a large role in the successful cases of natural childbirth, but like hypnosis, natural childbirth is not a method suitable for all women.

The latest method designed to eliminate labor pain is *abdominal decompression*, which has been employed for more than a decade in South Africa where it was invented and tested. Abdominal decompression reduces the atmospheric pressure outside the abdomen and is achieved by enclosing the woman's body from the chest down in a disposable, plastic stretch suit sealed at the upper chest. Then a button connected to a pump is pressed, creating the necessary negative pressure or vacuum. Usually one session of instruction before labor begins is enough to familiarize the woman with the technique and the resulting sensations, for she is asked to control both the degree and the duration of negative pressure during each contraction of labor. The decompression method has been reported not only to reduce the discomfort of labor, but also to shorten the entire labor process. It has been used in the United States to a limited extent, for obstetricians here are not convinced of its superiority over existing methods of relieving labor pain.

INDUCTION OF LABOR

The trend of the past fifteen years toward inducing labor applies to obstetrical-medical conditions, as well as to instances of convenience for both mother and physician.

Among the obstetrical-medical conditions for which induction is carried out are maternal diabetes, pyelonephritis, toxemia, Rh incompatibility, and premature separation of the placenta.

Obstetrics has come a long way since the time that quinine and castor oil were used for induction. There are newer, more powerful, and more controllable medical methods of induction today that are applied with greater selectivity, increasing skill, and safety. The two drugs currently used most frequently are *oxytocin*, a pituitary extract synthesized in 1953, and *sparteine*, a naturally occurring organic compound derived from plants.

Artificial induction of labor is also still accomplished by mechanical rupture of the membranes in certain cases. However, whether by medical or mechanical means, the timing of induction depends upon many factors which can only be determined by the obstetrician.

CERVIMETRY

It seems hard to believe that manual assessment of the degree of dilatation of the cervix in labor was not described in the medical literature until the early nineteenth century. Only just before the turn of the twentieth century was there a recommendation to assess the progress of the cervix, and therefore, of labor, by means of frequent rectal examination.

In the 1960's an electronic instrument, the electronic cervimeter, was designed to continuously measure and record the process of cervical dilatation. This instrument has a pair of arms which are introduced through the vagina and painlessly attached to the outer rim of the cervix. As the cervix dilates, the changes in relative positions of the two arms are recorded on a graph.

The electronic cervimeter has been used to shed further light on the physiology of labor, and although it is valuable for research purposes, it will probably never replace the manual method for following the course of labor.

INDUCTION OF MENSTRUATION AFTER DELIVERY

Artificial induction of labor and availability of the newer hormonal agents to suppress lactation have stimulated a new concept—to induce menstruation routinely six weeks after delivery.

Many women experience delays in resuming menstruation several weeks beyond this time, which gives rise to growing concern about the possibility that pregnancy has occurred so soon again. Induction of menstruation could be carried out in ninety percent of women by giving one of the birth control pills between the fourth and fifth week after giving birth.

17

Sexual Relations During and After Pregnancy

The problem of achieving sexual satisfaction during the entire cycle of pregnancy and following childbirth has been undergoing a reevaluation by the medical profession. In the past, standard textbooks in obstetrics-gynecology warned against sexual intercourse for every pregnant woman during the last six weeks of pregnancy and for six weeks after delivery. Today, with the exception of a few specific situations, most leading authorities no longer feel that this three-month period of abstinence is essential, or even beneficial, to the health of the mother and/or the unborn child. There is greater understanding that sexual intercourse is important to the marital relationship and to both marriage partners as they face prospective parenthood.

Like most other advice given to the pregnant woman regarding such concerns as diet, travel, and clothing, advice regarding sexual relations has to be tailored by the obstetrician to the specific needs and circumstances of both husband

and wife. They should feel free to ask any questions they may have about sexual activity during and after pregnancy.

THE NEED FOR SEXUAL RELATIONS DURING PREGNANCY

A woman who is pregnant, particularly for the first time, is subject to a number of anxieties concerning her general well-being, her physical attractiveness, and her husband's love. Many expectant mothers feel the need for an even closer physical relationship with their husbands; many, too, find sexual enjoyment greatly heightened, especially after the frequent fatigue and nausea of the first three months have passed. In the last three months of pregnancy, some women are not as interested in having intercourse, either because of some physical discomfort or for other reasons. However, for women whose sex drive remains undiminished, the feeling of being protected and loved is greatly enhanced by sexual fulfillment.

The husband of a pregnant woman is subject to counterpart distresses. The arbitrarily determined three-month period of sexual abstinence may create a hardship for him and may even jeopardize the marriage. According to Masters and Johnson, "many a male strays from the marital bed for the first time under these circumstances." On the other hand, many men report a lessening of their own sex drive near the end of their wives' pregnancies—sometimes due to needless fear that intercourse may harm the wife or the unborn child. A surprisingly large number of expectant fathers suffer from the same symptoms of pregnancy as their wives, and many even experience a postpartum depression, or "baby blues," after their child has been born.

WHEN SEXUAL RELATIONS ARE ALWAYS PROHIBITED

If there is vaginal bleeding at any time during pregnancy, sexual intercourse should be discontinued. Bleeding is of particular significance during the first three months when it could indicate a threatened abortion, and during the last three months when it could indicate an abnormally positioned placenta. The obstetrician should be called in all cases of vaginal bleeding.

In women with a history of previous miscarriages, some obstetricians may specify that intercourse should not take place at certain times (even though there is no definite proof that intercourse will result in interruption of pregnancy).

After the rupture of the membranes, all sexual activity should be stopped. Anything introduced into the vagina after the water has broken increases the danger of infection, posing a serious threat to the health of both mother and child.

Any pain, vaginal or abdominal, caused by intercourse should be reported to the obstetrician, who can advise when sexual relations may be continued.

After delivery, a woman should not engage in intercourse until bleeding has stopped, any incision (for episiotomy) has completely healed, and there is no discomfort in the genital area. For most women, this return to normal takes about three weeks.

PART IV

THE UNBORN CHILD

18

The Rh Factor

In 1930 Dr. Karl Landsteiner won the Nobel Prize in physiology and medicine for his discovery in 1900 of three of the four main types of human blood—A, B, AB, and O—initiating the current system of blood typing and infinitely safer blood transfusion. In 1940, together with Dr. Alexander Wiener, Dr. Landsteiner discovered the existence of a substance, or factor, in the red blood cells of human beings. It was named Rh from the species of monkey, *Macaca rhesus*, whose blood was found to contain a similar substance.

The Rh factor is present in the red blood cells of about eighty-five percent of the white population of the United States, who are termed "Rh positive." The remaining 15 percent, who do not have the Rh factor in their blood, are called "Rh negative." Less than five percent of Negroes have Rh negative blood, and among Orientals, Rh negative blood is virtually nonexistent.

Both the ABO and Rh factors—and therefore, blood types—are inherited and do not change throughout life. One's blood type is important to health only when blood must be transfused from one person to another, or during pregnancy, when the blood of the fetus is mixed with the blood of its mother. The Rh factor is antigenic—that is, it is able to produce an antibody response in people in whom this substance is absent and causes them to become sensitized. Under such circumstances, incompatible (or unmatched) bloods, when mixed, result in clumping and destruction of the sensitized red blood cells.

Until the recognition that the Rh factor could sensitize a mother's blood to that of her unborn child, Rh-positive red cells were sometimes introduced into an Rh-negative woman by a blood transfusion. Today Rh-negative women are given only Rh-negative blood to avoid this unnecessary sensitization. However, if a fetus has Rh-positive blood, its red cells may enter the circulation of its mother by way of the placenta during pregnancy or delivery. And if an Rh-negative woman receives Rh-positive cells, she *may* develop antibodies, or become Rh-sensitized. The mother's antibodies then pass through the placenta into the fetal circulation, where they may react with the Rh-positive blood of the fetus, causing destruction of its red blood cells and a severe anemia, jaundice, or even heart failure and brain damage. This group of abnormal conditions is termed Rh disease, or *erythroblastosis fetalis*, the name derived from large numbers of primitive red blood cells—erythroblasts—seen in the affected baby's blood. Normally, erythroblasts are found in bone marrow.

In severe cases of Rh disease, the fetus may die before birth or the newborn child may succumb at birth. If untreated, a baby with Rh disease may die within the first weeks of life. If both parents are Rh-negative, the infant has no problem. Erythroblastosis almost never occurs in a first pregnancy, even when the mother is Rh-negative and the baby is Rh-positive. However, subsequent pregnancies may be affected as the maternal antibodies continue to build up. In severe cases of Rh-sensitization, the second and all subsequent Rh-positive babies are affected. In milder cases, the second baby is not always affected, but the third or all later ones have problems.

Since the discovery of the Rh factor and its relation to erythroblastosis fetalis, efforts have been successfully directed to the earliest detection of Rh-sensitization of the mother and to the prevention, diagnosis, and treatment of the disease in infants.

DETECTING RH INCOMPATIBILITY

Early detection of Rh antibodies is accomplished by routine blood testing throughout pregnancy. The current approach is to see that all pregnant women at the first prenatal visit have their blood types determined and their blood screened for antibodies. The antibody screening is routinely repeated later in pregnancy.

If a mother is discovered to be Rh-negative, then her husband's blood type is also determined, and antibody screening of her blood is usually repeated at 28, 32, 36, and 40 weeks' gestation, and again six weeks after delivery.

Women who develop Rh-sensitivity have further routine blood tests to determine the type and amount of antibodies. The findings of these tests are used to help predict the likelihood that Rh disease will be a problem and to decide whether other diagnostic tests need to be done. If the buildup of antibodies reaches a dangerous level, then the obstetrician is faced with deciding upon the optimal time for delivery.*

Immediately following delivery of all infants, especially those of sensitized mothers, blood is taken from the umbilical cord for typing and for a special blood test called the Coombs test. The Coombs test shows whether or not the baby's blood

* Delivery is usually planned for between 34 and 35 weeks' gestation. Caesarean section used to be performed routinely, but vaginal delivery is now planned for, if labor can be safely induced.

cells are coated by its mother's antibodies. If they are coated, then a positive diagnosis of Rh disease can be made, even if the baby appears perfectly healthy. Then subsequent treatment of the baby can be planned.

If a previous baby had Rh disease and the present one has Rh-positive blood, it is almost certain to have Rh disease.

EXCHANGE TRANSFUSIONS

Equipment for exchange blood transfusions is now made ready when the birth of a baby with possible Rh damage is expected. In 1946 Dr. H. Wallerstein was the first to treat severe Rh disease by simultaneously removing the Rh-positive blood of the newborn infant and replacing it with Rh-negative blood. This procedure came to be safely performed and has been highly successful in saving the lives of babies born with Rh disease. Of course, it could only be applied to those infants who survived long enough *in utero* to be delivered alive.

In 1954 Doctors F. H. Allen, Jr., L. K. Diamond, and A. R. Jones proved that more babies could be salvaged if they could be rescued from the "hostile" environment of the uterus while they still had a chance to survive. By inducing labor (or performing a caesarean section) before term, the infant is delivered prematurely and can be given exchange transfusions earlier.

Exchange transfusion takes from one to two hours to perform and requires special equipment and specially trained hospital personnel. In replacement transfusion 10 to 20 cc. of the baby's blood is withdrawn from the umbilical cord and replaced immediately by whole Rh-negative blood. This procedure is repeated over and over again until approximately one pint of blood—or eighty-five to ninety percent of the infant's blood cells—has been removed and a similar amount has been replaced. Occasionally, additional exchange transfusions are required later.

AMNIOTIC FLUID EXAMINATION

While through the centuries people have marveled at the process of birth, they have been even more mystified by the unseen wonder of intrauterine life. There has long been a search for ways to find out more about the fetus before it is born. It was not until the middle of this century, however, that researchers devised one method—removing a small amount of amniotic fluid from the intact amniotic sac and examining its complex contents.

Early in pregnancy the embryo becomes surrounded by amniotic fluid enclosed in a membrane with two linings, the chorion or outermost covering, and the amnion, which is closer to the developing embryo. No one is quite sure of what contributes to the manufacture of amniotic fluid, which is ninety-eight percent water and two percent solid materials, such as protein, sugar, calcium, phosphorus, nitrogen, uric acid, adrenalin, carotene, citric acid, lactic acid, and pepsin. Amniotic fluid serves many purposes, both mechanical and biochemical. It acts as a protective cushion and pressure equalizer, and allows the fetus to shift its positions without sticking to the lining of the amniotic sac and uterus.

The amniotic fluid is the total environment of the fetus, which not only swallows the fluid, but also eliminates urine and meconium into it. Therefore, examination of the amniotic fluid offers a true chemical picture of fetal health throughout pregnancy.

Amniocentesis, the procedure by which the amniotic fluid is secured, is safe and simple when performed by experienced hands. After the mother's bladder is emptied and the fetal position and heart sounds are checked, a tiny needle is inserted into the uterus through the abdomen or cervix, and a small amount (5 to 20 cc.) of fluid removed from the amniotic sac. Neither sedation nor local anaesthesia is generally required. The woman is observed about an hour before being sent home. In the management of Rh disease, amniocentesis is usually first performed at about 28–29 weeks gestation and repeated at intervals until delivery.

Amniotic fluid analysis has contributed to a marked reduction in fetal loss due to Rh disease because it has enabled the obstetrician to determine with accuracy when and when not to induce labor, and when a fetus may require intrauterine transfusions (discussed in the following section). The development of amniocentesis and the subsequent amniotic fluid analysis have opened a new horizon for the study of life within the uterus, making it possible to determine many other facets of the health of both fetus and mother. Chemical and cellular analyses of amniotic fluid have been used to indicate fetal distress, to detect hereditary disorders, to determine the fetal blood type—and even the sex of the fetus.

Two other new techniques for examining amniotic fluid are amniography and amnioscopy. In amniography, a radiopaque material is injected into the amniotic fluid for X-ray studies of the fetus, the placenta, and the umbilical cord. The position of the fetus is clearly seen, and even its gastrointestinal tract is outlined because the fetus swallows the radiopaque material in the amniotic fluid. (This is of great importance in locating the proper place to inject the needle in giving a fetus an intrauterine transfusion.) The diagnosis of the sex of a male fetus can be made in those instances when the penis and scrotum are clearly identified. (Occasionally a fetus can be seen sucking its thumb.) Amniography is extremely helpful in determining the extent of Rh disease and can also be used to disclose abnormalities of the uterus and to diagnose special medical problems of the fetus and mother.

In amnioscopy, an instrument with a light attached is inserted into the cervix to illuminate and allow observation of the lower portion of the amniotic membranes, the amniotic fluid itself, and the fetus. This procedure is used in Rh disease to determine if the amniotic fluid is of a normal color, or if Rh disease has progressed to such a state that abnormal pigment is present. If the color of the fluid is normal, the obstetrician may regard amniocentesis as unnecessary. However, if amniotic fluid appears bile-stained, he will probably do an amniocentesis and have the amniotic fluid analyzed.

INTRAUTERINE TRANSFUSION

In 1963, Dr. A. W. Liley of the University of Auckland, New Zealand, gave the first successful blood transfusion to a severely anemic Rh-positive male fetus who most certainly would otherwise have died before it could have been delivered. This event ushered in a new era in the treatment of severe Rh disease, and since that time, thousands of lifesaving intrauterine transfusions have been performed.

Intrauterine transfusion takes about one and one-half hours to perform. The mother is sedated and given a local anaesthetic. Then the doctor injects up to five ounces of concentrated Rh-negative red blood cells through the mother's abdomen and uterine wall into the baby's abdominal cavity, from which these red blood cells are later absorbed into its circulation. Depending upon the condition of the fetus, this procedure may be repeated before the infant is born.

Approximately ten percent of all Rh-negative mothers become sensitized and only about half of them carry babies ill enough with Rh disease to require amniocentesis. Of this group, only about one or two babies out of seven or eight will require intrauterine transfusion. The risk inherent in the procedure of transfusing an unborn baby is low, and the results can be dramatically effective.

ABO INCOMPATIBILITY

In 1944 it was first recognized that erythroblastosis fetalis could also be caused by incompatibility of A, B, and O blood groups between mother and fetus. When the mother is type O and the father is type A or B, the fetus inherits its father's blood type, as A and B genes are dominant over O. The mother's blood contains natural antibodies to the other blood types, and should it cross the placental barrier and attack the infant's red blood cells, ABO sensitization takes place.

As in Rh disease, ABO disease may occur in a first pregnancy, but its presence and severity are unpredictable in subsequent pregnancies. Furthermore, ABO disease is much milder than Rh disease, the most adverse effect on the baby usually being jaundice. Infants who are likely to develop jaundice to a dangerous degree are treated by exchange transfusion. Fortunately, exchange transfusion for ABO disease is required less than once in 1,000 deliveries.

PREVENTION OF RH DISEASE

The 1960's have witnessed an advance in the prevention of Rh disease that promises to virtually eliminate the entire problem of Rh sensitization within a generation. While this medical achievement has arrived too late to help more than a million currently sensitized American women of childbearing age, within a decade Rh disease may become a rarity in areas where modern medicine is practiced.

The principle of this new approach and its application are simple. The Rh-negative mother who has delivered an Rh-positive infant receives a single injection of a blood product called *Rh immunoglobulin*—gamma globulin containing large quantities of anti-Rh antibodies. This is given usually within twenty-four hours after birth to prevent the mother from becoming sensitized by her baby's Rh-positive blood and later producing antibodies that could attack a future Rh-positive fetus.

Rh immunoglobulin has a very recent history. In 1960 an American research team—Drs. Vincent Freda, John G. Gorman, and William Pollack—began working on a way to prevent Rh disease, using a principle of immunization that dates back to 1909. Almost at the same time, Dr. Ronald Finn and Dr. Cyril Clarke of Liverpool, England, began their own Rh research, using the same immunological principle. After many experiments by both teams, the Americans developed a preparation of gamma globulin having a high concentration of anti-Rh antibodies and began clinical trials on mothers in 1964. Soon there were clinical trials in England, Scotland, and West

Germany. The results of these trials proved this method to be nearly 100 percent effective, with no significant harmful effects on either the mother or infant.

It now appears foreseeable that the single Rh immunoglobulin injection will one day make obsolete the need for such ingenious and daring techniques as amniocentesis and intrauterine transfusion.

19

Birth Defects

All parents want perfect children, and fortunately, about ninety-five percent of all babies born to parents in the United States are normal. However, about five percent of infants are born with minor to severe birth defects, ranging from color blindness to hydrocephalus and other abnormalities of the central nervous system. Hundreds of thousands more pregnancies each year end in stillbirth or miscarriage.

Birth defects, or *congenital* malformations (congenital means "present at birth"), may be inherited or may be the result of a number of circumstances occurring during intrauterine fetal development. These include diseases in the mother during pregnancy, drugs taken early in pregnancy, and excessive radiation. Maternal aging is a factor in at least one abnormality, Down's syndrome (formerly called mongolism). Birth order is considered significant in congenital dislocation of the hip and certain other defects. Mechanical stress or pressure on the fetus in utero is still thought to be one cause of clubfoot and other malformations.

THE GENETIC COUNSELOR

One of the greatest scientific accomplishments in recent years has been the piecing together of one of mankind's oldest puzzles—the mechanism of human heredity and how it affects physical and mental health. Two decades ago several hundred disorders were known to be caused by hereditary defects. Today there are more than 1,500 ailments (most of them rare) recognized as stemming from genetic abnormalities.

From the newly developed and complex science of human genetics has come a new type of health specialist—the genetic counselor. He may or may not be a physician, but he has had graduate training in medical genetics. His prime function is to provide people with an understanding of the potential genetic problems that exist in their families, and to guide couples in making major decisions about marriage and parenthood in an effort to prevent heritable disorders from being transmitted.

The genetic counselor will ask the parents of a defective child, for example, such questions as: Have the parents had normal children before the one being evaluated? Did the father have diagnostic or therapeutic radiation? What is the pregnancy history of the mother—number of miscarriages, stillbirths, and infant deaths? During the pregnancy was there rubella or other viral diseases, toxemia, anemia, bleeding, radiation, drugs? Is there a history of prematurity, postmaturity, or fetal maternal blood group incompatibility? Age of the parents, the medical history of other relatives, and evidence of blood relationship are also of extreme importance to the genetic counselor.

For centuries, folklore and superstition attributed birth defects to such imagined causes as evil spirits, lewd thoughts, fornication with animals, or other immoral or unnatural acts. It was commonplace to hold up to public criticism and ridicule the mother and/or father of a malformed infant. Modern genetics, however, has shown that *everyone* carries an average of five to ten abnormal genes, although not necessarily affected by any one of them. It is an unfortunate coincidence when two people carrying the same hidden gene defect become parents of an obviously affected child.

CHROMOSOMES AND GENES

It was only one hundred years ago that the Austrian monk Gregor Mendel first formulated the fundamental laws of genetics, based, among other things, upon his observations and experiments in growing garden peas. The Mendelian laws of heredity have been shown to apply to human heredity and have been the basis for the science of human genetics that has evolved so rapidly since 1950. It was not until 1956, in fact, that the correct number of man's chromosomes was finally agreed upon.

The biological uniqueness of each embryo, fetus, child, and finally each adult at any time during his existence is due to the chromosomal and genetic inheritance which he originally received, and to the nature of the environment in which he has existed until that time. From the moment when the father's sperm and the mother's ovum unite to form the single cell that begins the life of a new human being, basic characteristics of that individual are determined. Genetic "information" contained in this cell is like a blueprint specifying how the new person will be constructed, from facial features and coloring to size and shape—even chemical functioning and mental capacity. The first cell divides and multiplies, and all subsequent cells contain not only the same genetic makeup, but also everything needed to carry out their future special functions, such as making blood, bone, muscle, skin, and hair and forming such diverse organs as the brain, kidney, heart, lung, and sex glands.

In the nucleus of every single human cell are forty-six threadlike particles, the chromosomes. Every chromosome is composed of hundreds and perhaps thousands of genes, the basic units of heredity. The forty-six chromosomes consist of twenty-three pairs, one member of each pair having come from the father, the other from the mother. Of the twenty-three pairs, twenty-two are called the autosomes, and the other pair the sex chromosomes, for indeed, they alone determine the genetic sex of the individual. Like chromosomes, genes occur in pairs—one of each pair deriving from each parent.

The Mendelian theory has led to the discovery of patterns of the inheritance of disease in man. Genetic defects may be responsible for miscarriages, fetal deaths in the womb, deaths at or shortly after delivery, abnormalities discovered at birth, and illnesses developing at any time of life. Genetic defects may also be responsible for mild or completely controllable conditions. In addition, a person may carry an inherited gene defect without his being affected, yet he may pass it along to the next generation. The wide range of immediate and remote effects of defective genes depends in part on the special function of the affected genes, as well as the way they are inherited.

The manner of inheritance depends upon whether the abnormal gene is *dominant* or *recessive* with respect to its normal gene counterpart, or whether it is attached to the sex chromosome, and therefore, *sex-linked*. Usually, disorders inherited in a dominant manner are transmitted by a single abnormal gene from either parent. The gene is called dominant because it dominates its normal partner and produces disease. The probability is fifty percent that any individual child of an affected parent will be similarly affected. However, if the child does not inherit the condition, his offspring will usually be free of it forever.

Sometimes an abnormality can be transmitted to a child only when it receives a pair of abnormal genes, one coming from each parent. Such an inheritance is called recessive because, in contrast to the dominant trait which results in disease when only one gene is abnormal, no disease results if only one abnormal gene is present. Parents of a child with a recessively inherited disease run a twenty-five percent risk that each subsequent child may be similarly affected.

When the sex chromosome carries an abnormal gene, sex-linked (or X-linked) recessive inheritance may occur. The normal male has one X chromosome, and his sex chromosome constitution is XY. The normal female has two X chromosomes, and her chromosome constitution is XX. *The defective gene is attached to the X chromosome.* Usually, only men are affected by X-linked disease and pass the defect on to their daughters, all of whom become carriers. Women carriers are usually not affected by the disease, but transmit it to half their sons. It is rare for a woman to be afflicted by a sex-linked genetic disease, but this could happen if a woman carrier marries a man with a sex-linked genetic disease.

There are additional modes of inheritance too complex to be so simply analyzed, partially because many traits and characteristics may be determined by combinations of genes, as well as by multitudes of environmental influences acting on the unborn child.

GENETIC DISORDERS

From biblical times, man has observed that physical and mental abnormalities, as well as characteristics of appearance and personality, are frequently transmitted from parents to offspring down through the generations. The Bible itself advises against certain unions of blood relatives for just this reason. Hippocrates described the recurrence of such traits as crossed eyes, bald-headedness, epilepsy, and a particular kind of blindness in certain families. In spite of this early astute concept of hereditary disease, more than two thousand years were to pass before interest in the hereditary transmission of human disease was revived and the science of human genetics was born. While the most obvious physical deformities, such as having extra fingers or toes, were recognized at birth, only in recent times have there been explanations of how genetic abnormalities could show up during childhood, adolescence, adulthood, and even in old age.

Among the apparent genetic defects seen at birth are harelip, cleft palate, clubfoot, and dislocation of the hip—all of which can be repaired surgically. There are, however, many rare conditions such as malformations of the central nervous system that are incompatible with life and can be fatal in a matter of days or months.

Down's syndrome (the condition formerly referred to as mongolism) is usually recognizable at birth or within a few months. It is characterized by varying degrees of mental retardation along with certain physical features, including an Oriental-like folding of the upper inner eyelids. Down's syndrome can be inherited or can be due to some "accident" of chromosomal rearrangement during the process of conception. A genetic counselor is able to determine by thorough family histories and laboratory analysis of an afflicted child whether the defect was hereditary or not, and therefore, whether or not the parents stand a great or very slight risk of having another abnormal baby. It is estimated that Down's syndrome occurs once in six hundred births, accounting for nearly six thousand defective infants every year.

A relatively rare sex-linked hereditary disease that becomes apparent during childhood is hemophilia, the "bleeder's disease," so called because it is characterized by a tendency to uncontrollable bleeding, even after a minor injury. Although only one boy in 10,000 is born with some form of hemophilia, the danger of hemorrhage and the need for emergency transfusions have dramatized the plight of those afflicted. Hemophiliac bleeding is currently treated with transfusion of fresh whole blood, fresh frozen plasma, or AHG (anti-hemophilic globulin), a special concentrate of blood plasma. Up until the 1950's, hemophilia had not been reported in females, but since that time a few women have been proven to be victims of the disease.

Probably the most common of all inherited diseases is diabetes mellitus, whose onset can range from early childhood to extreme old age. It is estimated that more than four million Americans have diabetes, and that one person in four carries the gene. The main reason for this is that diabetics have been helped by modern medicine to conceive and bear living children, all of whom are potential carriers.

Hundreds of other genetic disorders, such as Huntington's

chorea, Wilson's disease, Klinefelter's syndrome, galactosemia, and phenylketonuria, are comparatively rare. But these and other genetic diseases afflict an unfortunately large number of children and adults who suffer various degrees of illness or handicap or both.

GENETIC COUNSELING SERVICES

In addition to predicting what hazards there might be for a future child, genetic counseling serves many other helpful functions. Genetic counselors can advise parents on the problems of raising one or more healthy children with the added burden of a defective child in the family. In addition, they are able to advise on such matters as adoption, institutionalization, finances and sources of aid, sterilization, abortion, and even artificial insemination.

Until recently, there were few centers to which physicians could refer concerned couples. Now there are well over one hundred facilities for genetic counseling throughout the country, as listed on the following pages, and more are being continually set up. There are also some one hundred birth-defect centers now financed by The National Foundation–March of Dimes that include genetic counseling as an integral part of their services.

It is the ultimate goal of geneticists to detect and be able to eliminate undesirable genes in order to prevent the transmission of inherited diseases and disorders, thereby improving man's genetic endowment.

GENETIC COUNSELING SERVICES IN THE UNITED STATES*

STATE	CITY	COUNSELING FACILITY
Alabama	Birmingham	University of Alabama Medical Center (Laboratory of Medical Genetics)
Alaska	College	Arctic Health Research Laboratory
Arizona	Tempe	Arizona State University (Department of Zoology)
Arkansas	Little Rock	University of Arkansas Medical Center (Birth Defects Center)
California	Berkeley	University of California (Departments of Zoology & Genetics)
	Duarte	City of Hope Medical Center (Department of Medical Genetics)
	Irvine	University of California at Irvine (Department of Pediatrics)
	Los Angeles	Children's Hospital (Departments of Pediatrics & Biochemistry)

* Adapted from *International Directory of Genetic Services*, edited by Daniel Bergsma, M.D., Henry T. Lynch, M.D., Anne J. Krush, M.S., and Rev. Edward A. Sharp, S.J., and published by The National Foundation—March of Dimes, 1968.

STATE	CITY	COUNSELING FACILITY
	Los Angeles	University of California Center for Health Sciences (Departments of Pediatrics & Medicine)
	Los Angeles	University of Southern California Medical Center
	Martinez	Genetics Consultation & Counseling Service (Department of Health)
	Oakland	Children's Hospital Medical Center (Department of Birth Defects)
	Palo Alto	Palo Alto Stanford Hospital (Department of Pediatrics)
	Palo Alto	Stanford University School of Medicine (Department of Medicine)
	San Bernardino	St. Bernadine's Hospital (Department of Pediatrics)
	San Francisco	Children's Hospital (Adult Medical Center)
	San Francisco	University of California (Department of Pediatrics)
	San Francisco	University of California Medical Center (Department of Pediatrics)
Colorado	Denver	University of Colorado Medical Center (Departments of Pediatrics & Biophysics)
Connecticut	Hartford	Connecticut Twin Registry (Department of Health)

STATE	CITY	COUNSELING FACILITY
	New Haven	Yale University School of Medicine (Department of Pediatrics)
	Ridgefield	New England Institute for Medical Research (Department of Cytogenetics)
District of Columbia (Washington, D.C.)		Children's Hospital (Department of Neurology)
		Georgetown University Hospital (Departments of Pediatrics & Obstetrics)
		Howard University College of Medicine (Department of Medical Genetics)
		The George Washington University Hospital (Departments of Obstetrics & Gynecology)
Florida	Miami	University of Miami Child Development Center (Department of Pediatrics)
Georgia	Atlanta	Georgia Mental Health Institute (Department of Psychiatry, Emory University)
	Augusta	Medical College of Georgia (Departments of Endocrinology & Pediatrics)
	Milledgeville	Central State Hospital

STATE	CITY	COUNSELING FACILITY
Hawaii	Honolulu	Kauikeolani Children's Hospital (Department of Birth Defects)
Illinois	Chicago	Children's Hospital (Department of Biochemistry)
	Chicago	Illinois State Pediatric Institute
	Chicago	Michael Reese Research Foundation (Blood Center)
	Chicago	Mount Sinai Hospital Medical Center (Department of Experimental Pathology)
	Chicago	The University of Chicago (Departments of Medicine & Pediatrics)
	Evanston	Evanston Hospital (Department of Research)
	Springfield	Department of Public Health (Division of Preventive Medicine)
Indiana	Indianapolis	Indiana University Medical School (Department of Medical Genetics)
Iowa	Iowa City	University Hospitals (Department of Pediatrics)
Kansas	Kansas City	Kansas University Medical Center (Department of Medicine)

STATE	CITY	COUNSELING FACILITY
	Wichita	Wesley Medical Research Foundation (Department of Clinical Pathology)
Kentucky	Lexington	University of Kentucky Medical Center (Department of Pediatrics)
	Louisville	Child Evaluation Center (Department of Pediatrics)
	Louisville	University of Louisville School of Medicine (Department of Pediatrics)
Louisiana	New Orleans	Tulane University (Department of Anatomy)
Maryland	Baltimore	The Johns Hopkins Hospital (The Moore Clinic)
	Baltimore	Sinai Hospital (Department of Pediatrics)
Massachusetts	Boston	Birth Defects Center
	Boston	Children's Hospital Medical Center (Clinical Genetics Division)
	Boston	Massachusetts General Hospital (Departments of Medicine & Pediatrics)
Michigan	Ann Arbor	University of Michigan (Department of Human Genetics)

STATE	CITY	COUNSELING FACILITY
	Detroit	Henry Ford Hospital (Department of Pediatrics)
	Detroit	University of Detroit (Department of Biology)
	Grand Rapids	Butterworth Hospital (Department of Pediatric Neurology)
	Lansing	Michigan State University (Department of Zoology)
	Northville	Plymouth State Home & Training School (Department of Mental Health)
Minnesota	Minneapolis	Minnesota Department of Health (Department of Human Genetics)
	Minneapolis	University of Minnesota (Department of Genetics)
	Minneapolis	University of Minnesota Dental School (School of Dentistry)
Mississippi	Jackson	University of Mississippi Medical Center (Department of Preventive Medicine)
Missouri	Columbia	University of Missouri Medical Center (Department of Pediatrics)
	St. Louis	Children's Hospital (Department of Pediatrics)
	St. Louis	St. Louis University (Department of Pediatrics)

STATE	CITY	COUNSELING FACILITY
	St. Louis	Washington University (Departments of Medicine & Pediatrics)
	St. Louis	Washington University Medical School (Department of Medicine)
Nebraska	Omaha	Children's Memorial Hospital (Birth Defects Clinic)
	Omaha	The Creighton University School of Medicine (Department of Preventive Medicine)
New Hampshire	Hanover	Dartmouth Medical School (Departments of Pathology & Medicine)
New Jersey	Newark	New Jersey College of Medicine, Newark City Hospital (Department of Pediatrics)
New Mexico	Albuquerque	University of New Mexico School of Medicine (Department of Pathology)
New York	Albany	Birth Defects Institute, Albany Medical College (New York State Department of Health)
	Buffalo	Buffalo General Hospital (Department of Medicine)

STATE	CITY	COUNSELING FACILITY
	Buffalo	New York University at Buffalo (Department of Pediatrics)
	Buffalo	State University of New York at Buffalo (Department of Pediatrics)
	Jamaica	Creedmoor State Hospital (Medical Service Division)
	Manhasset	North Shore Hospital (Genetics Laboratory)
	New York (Bronx)	Albert Einstein College of Medicine of Yeshiva University (Departments of Genetics & Medicine)
	New York	Mount Sinai School of Medicine (Department of Pediatrics)
	New York	The New York Blood Center
	New York	New York Medical College, Metropolitan Hospital
	New York	New York State Psychiatric Institute (Department of Medical Genetics)
	New York	New York University Medical Center
	New York	St. Luke's Hospital Center
	Rochester	Rochester University Medical School (Division of Genetics)
	Syracuse	Upstate Medical Center (Department of Pediatrics)
North Carolina	Chapel Hill	Birth Defects Clinic (Department of Pediatrics)

STATE	CITY	COUNSELING FACILITY
	Morganton	Western Carolina Center (Birth Defects Evaluation Clinic)
Ohio	Cincinnati	Children's Hospital Research Foundation (Department of Pediatrics)
	Cleveland	Case Western Reserve University School of Medicine, Cleveland Metropolitan General Hospital
	Cleveland	Cleveland Psychiatric Institute (Department of Medical Genetics)
	Columbus	Children's Hospital (Department of Pediatrics)
	Columbus	University Hospital (Department of Medicine)
	Dayton	Barney Children's Medical Center (Birth Defects Evaluation Center)
Oklahoma	Oklahoma City	Children's Hospital (Department of Pediatrics)
Oregon	Eugene	Sacred Heart Hospital (Department of Pediatrics)
	Portland	University of Oregon Medical School (General Clinic, Crippled Children's Division)
Pennsylvania	Danville	Geisinger Medical Center (Department of Pathology)

STATE	CITY	COUNSELING FACILITY
	Philadelphia	Children's Hospital (Department of Pediatrics)
	Philadelphia	Hahnemann Medical College (Department of Anatomy)
	Philadelphia	Jefferson Hospital (Department of Medicine)
	Pittsburgh	Children's Hospital
Rhode Island	Providence	Rhode Island Hospital (Department of Pediatrics)
Tennessee	Knoxville	University of Tennessee (Birth Defects Evaluation Center)
	Memphis	University of Tennessee (Department of Pediatrics)
	Nashville	Meharry Medical College (Department of Pediatrics)
	Nashville	Vanderbilt Hospital (Department of Medicine)
Texas	Austin	The Genetics Foundation (Department of Human Genetic Research)
	Fort Sam Houston	Brooke General Hospital
	Galveston	University of Texas Medical Branch (Department of Human Genetics)
	Houston	Baylor University College of Medicine (Department of Pediatrics)
	Houston	M. D. Anderson Hospital (Department of Biology)

STATE	CITY	COUNSELING FACILITY
	Pasadena	Pasadena General Hospital (Department of Medical Genetics)
	San Antonio	University of Texas Medical School (Department of Anatomy)
Utah	Logan	Utah State University (Department of Zoology)
	Salt Lake City	Primary Children's Hospital (Birth Defects Clinic)
	Salt Lake City	University Medical Center (Department of Internal Medicine)
Vermont	Burlington	Mary Fletcher Hospital (Department of Pediatrics)
Virginia	Charlottesville	University of Virginia Hospital (Department of Internal Medicine)
	Charlottesville	University of Virginia School of Medicine (Chromosome Research Laboratory)
	Richmond	Medical College of Virginia (Departments of Biology & Genetics)
Washington	Seattle	University of Washington (Department of Medicine)
West Virginia	Morgantown	West Virginia University Hospital (Department of Pediatrics)

STATE	CITY	COUNSELING FACILITY
Wisconsin	Madison	University of Wisconsin Medical School (Department of Medical Genetics)
	Milwaukee	The Milwaukee Children's Hospital (Cytogenetics Laboratory & Genetics Clinic)

DEFECTS DUE TO DRUGS

The human embryo is fortunately and remarkably well-protected from the ill effects of most drugs. Up until the thalidomide tragedy of 1961, only a few cases of malformations in human infants had been attributed to drugs taken by the mother during her pregnancy—namely, aminopterin and certain hormones. Others, such as quinine, had been reported to cause deafness of the infant as well as disorders of the blood. However, the discovery that thalidomide taken in the first trimester of pregnancy caused certain types of skeletal and other abnormalities has led to the cautious use of all drugs in the first three months of pregnancy.

Originally introduced in West Germany in 1956 under the proprietary name of Grippex, thalidomide was at first thought to be effective against influenza. It was later found to have a sedative effect in man, and after some experimental testing, it was prematurely released for sale to the public as Contergan, a highly effective new sleeping pill with an amazing absence of acute toxicity even in high doses. Approximately eight thousand couples in different parts of the world were left with dead or crippled children in the wake of thalidomide, which subsequently was withdrawn from the market. It had never been allowed to be marketed in the United States. However, some thalidomide had been distributed to American doctors for experimental use and some had been brought back to the United States by returning tourists, resulting in at least four cases of malformed infants born to American parents, including a set of deformed twins.

The case of Mrs. Sherri Finkbine, who had taken thalidomide in early pregnancy and was refused an abortion by the Superior Court of Arizona—in spite of a three-member panel of physicians who advised her to have an abortion—brought worldwide attention to the rigid American abortion laws. Mrs. Finkbine was forced to secure an abortion out of the country and the fetus she was carrying was shown to have been severely deformed.

There is now evidence that lysergic acid diethylamide—LSD—can produce cellular changes in the fetus of a woman who takes the hallucinogenic drug. LSD has been shown to produce chromosomal aberrations similar to those noted in three autosomal recessive diseases, including a form of leukemia. Since the results of such genetic defects may not appear for a generation or more, it is too early to determine the extent of adverse effects LSD may have on future offspring of today's LSD users.

DEFECTS DUE TO DISEASE

Rubella, formerly called German measles, is a viral disease that usually produces mild symptoms in the person in whom it occurs. However, when it occurs in a pregnant woman, the virus, like thalidomide, is likely to damage the unborn child, especially during the first trimester of pregnancy. Rubella epidemics occur in somewhat predictable cycles about every seven years. The last rubella epidemic in the United States in 1963–64 resulted in tens of thousands of defective children.

In 1940 there was an extensive and severe epidemic of rubella in Australia. As the country was at war, many young adults of both sexes called up for war service were housed or worked under conditions that contribute to the spread of epidemic disease. In 1941 there was a dramatically increased number of babies born with congenital malformations. That year Dr. Norman McAlister Gregg, an eye specialist of Sydney, presented at a meeting of ophthalmologists a paper entitled "Congenital Cataract Following German Measles in the Mother," which was the first documented recognition of the association between a virus infection in a mother and defects in her fetus.

Since this discovery, the rubella virus has been proven to cause numerous defects in the majority of infants born to mothers infected during the first three months of pregnancy. It has been observed that the earlier the disease occurs in the mother, the greater the risk to the baby. In general, rubella in the mother who is five to eight weeks pregnant tends to produce congenital cataract, from seven to twelve weeks congenital heart malformations, and from four to nine weeks congenital deafness. Liver enlargement, jaundice, skeletal malformations, small head size, mental retardation, glaucoma, and other defects have been attributed to the rubella virus in recent epidemics.

In the middle of the 1950's, a new and contagious form of rubella was discovered—rubella syndrome, or congenital rubella. During the course of maternal rubella, the embryo and placenta become heavily infected with the virus, with the result that an aborted embryo, a stillborn fetus, or even an apparently healthy newborn infant can carry the rubella virus and serve as a source of contagion. The virus can be excreted in the baby's urine and stool, and can also be carried in the baby's eyes, nasal passages, and throat—for as long as six or more months after birth. Until the rubella virus eventually disappears, these babies can spread the infection to susceptible women who take care of them.

Within the past few years, maternal rubella during the second trimester of pregnancy has also been found to adversely affect the infant. Although the subsequent defects tend to be less severe than those produced during the first trimester, such conditions as mental retardation, deafness, growth failure, and jaundice have resulted.

The rubella virus was first isolated as recently as 1962. This isolation led to the development in 1966 by Drs. Harry M.

Meyer, Jr., and Paul D. Parkman, of the National Institutes of Health, of a blood test for rubella antibodies. This test can help to determine more definitely whether a rash developing during early pregnancy was indeed due to rubella, and can thus place on firmer ground a medical decision regarding the need for therapeutic abortion. The following year, this same team of doctors developed a vaccine for rubella that is currently being field-tested. The results of field trials during a 1968 rubella epidemic in Taiwan proved the vaccine to be highly protective. This is the basis of the hope that by 1970, when another epidemic of rubella is expected in the United States, a safe and effective vaccine will be available to prevent thousands of unborn children from being attacked by the disease.

The rubella story has opened the eyes of the medical world to the possible interrelations of other maternal virus infections to fetal wastage and defective infants—among those, influenza, polio, Coxsackie virus, and cytomegalovirus. The precise statistical consequences of a specific viral disease in pregnancy have yet to be calculated. However, in no instance does the likelihood of damage to a new life in utero from any other virus appear to approach the magnitude of the rubella relationship.

PART V

THE NEWBORN CHILD

20

The Transition from Fetus to Newborn

The most visibly dramatic moment in life, and perhaps the most hazardous, is the moment of birth. Successful transition from intrauterine life to independent existence in "extrauterine life" depends upon the infant's ability to adapt itself rapidly to its radically altered environment. Its supply of oxygen must no longer come from the placenta but from its lungs; the waste products of its metabolism can no longer be eliminated by the mother, but must suddenly be handled by the infant's internal organs; the infant must now control its own delicate fluid balance and body temperature. Failure to make these vital adjustments would result in death soon after birth. Other functions that the newborn child has to assume without delay are those of nourishment and defense against harmful agents in the new environment (mainly viruses and bacteria).

The world is witnessing the birth of a new era in obstetrics and pediatrics—the era of the fetus and the newborn. Special attention is being paid to those babies whose obstetrical histories indicate that they will be likely to have difficulty surviving the first few days of life. In addition, physicians are making great strides in the early diagnosis and prompt treatment of birth defects and congenital illnesses that threaten life in the newborn, using many new imaginative techniques.

In 1967 in the United States, infant mortality—infants dying before one year of age—dropped to a new low of 22 per 1,000 live births. (At the turn of the century, the infant mortality rate in this country was 162.4 per 1,000 births.) Despite the fact that a greater percentage of American babies are surviving infancy than ever before, the decrease in infant mortality has slowed down since 1950. The highest rate of infant deaths today is found in economically and socially disadvantaged groups. Not until more and better health care facilities are made available to these underprivileged mothers will the United States be able to make significant further reductions in infant mortality. In the meantime, the ingenuity of modern medicine is being increasingly applied to the awesome miracle of birth.

FETAL BLOOD SAMPLING

Introduced in 1966, fetal blood sampling is an important technique that offers a direct method of determining the well-being of a fetus during labor and delivery. A small amount of the fetus' capillary blood is withdrawn from its scalp during labor by means of an amnioscope inserted into the mother's vagina. The blood sample is then tested for acidity (pH), and often for its oxygen and carbon dioxide content—reflections of the amount of metabolic stress being placed on the infant. If the stress is great enough to jeopardize the infant's life, immediate delivery is performed.

This extraordinary new type of blood test is done early in labor when there are signs of fetal distress, and in the presence of such pregnancy complications as diabetes, toxemia, Rh sensitization, and postmaturity (when the baby is overdue). Fetal blood sampling is often done in cases where a woman has a history of previous stillbirths or other types of reproductive failure. In spite of the dramatic way in which the blood sample is taken, fetal blood sampling is safe for both mother and child and is relatively simple to perform.

APGAR TEST

Since 1953, when Dr. Virginia Apgar first published a description of her five-step method of determining the health of newborn infants *one minute after birth*, the "Apgar test" has become a standard procedure used around the world.

EPIGRAM OF THE APGAR SCORE*

	SIGN	POINTS		
		0	1	2
A	APPEARANCE (color)	blue pale	body pink extremities blue	completely pink
P	PULSE (heart rate)	absent	below 100	over 100
G	GRIMACE (reflex irritability response to stimulation of sole of foot)	no response	grimace	cry
A	ACTIVITY (muscle tone)	limp	some flexion of extremities	active motion
R	RESPIRATION (respiratory effort)	absent	slow irregular	good strong cry

* Originated by Dr. Joseph Butterfield, The Newborn Center, The Children's Hospital, Denver, Colorado.

Only a few seconds are needed to perform the test, which yields a rating or "score" for the individual infant. The test is then repeated in four minutes.

The appearance of the baby (color of the lips, palms, soles, trunk, and extremities) is observed first. Then the pulse, or heart rate, is determined. The child's grimace, or facial expression in response to stimulation of the soles of the feet or to tickling of the inside of the nose, is then noted. Activity, or muscle tone, is evaluated next, followed by observation of respiration, or respiratory effort.

Approximately fifteen percent of babies achieve the best possible score of ten. A baby with a score of seven or less is considered a "risk" and is observed carefully until its functions improve. A score of four or less indicates that a baby needs immediate resuscitation. With prompt attention, even a zero-rated infant, according to Dr. Apgar, stands a better than fifty percent chance of surviving.

THE LOW BIRTH WEIGHT INFANT AND PREMATURITY

Recent research has led during the past few years to changes in the terminology regarding newborns in relation to their size and development at birth. The term *premature* had formerly been used to refer to newborn infants weighing 5½ lb. or less at birth *or* with a gestational period of less than 37 weeks. Today babies of 5½ lb. or under are termed *low birth weight* infants, and *premature* babies are those born before the completion of 37 weeks' gestation.

There are a number of babies who are small at birth but who have had a gestation period of normal length. Referred to as "small for dates," these infants can be healthy babies who are small for genetic reasons and may have small parents, or they may be under normal weight because of possible malnutrition during pregnancy, sometimes associated with the presumed placental "insufficiency" of toxemia.

Prematurity, the leading cause of infant death in the United

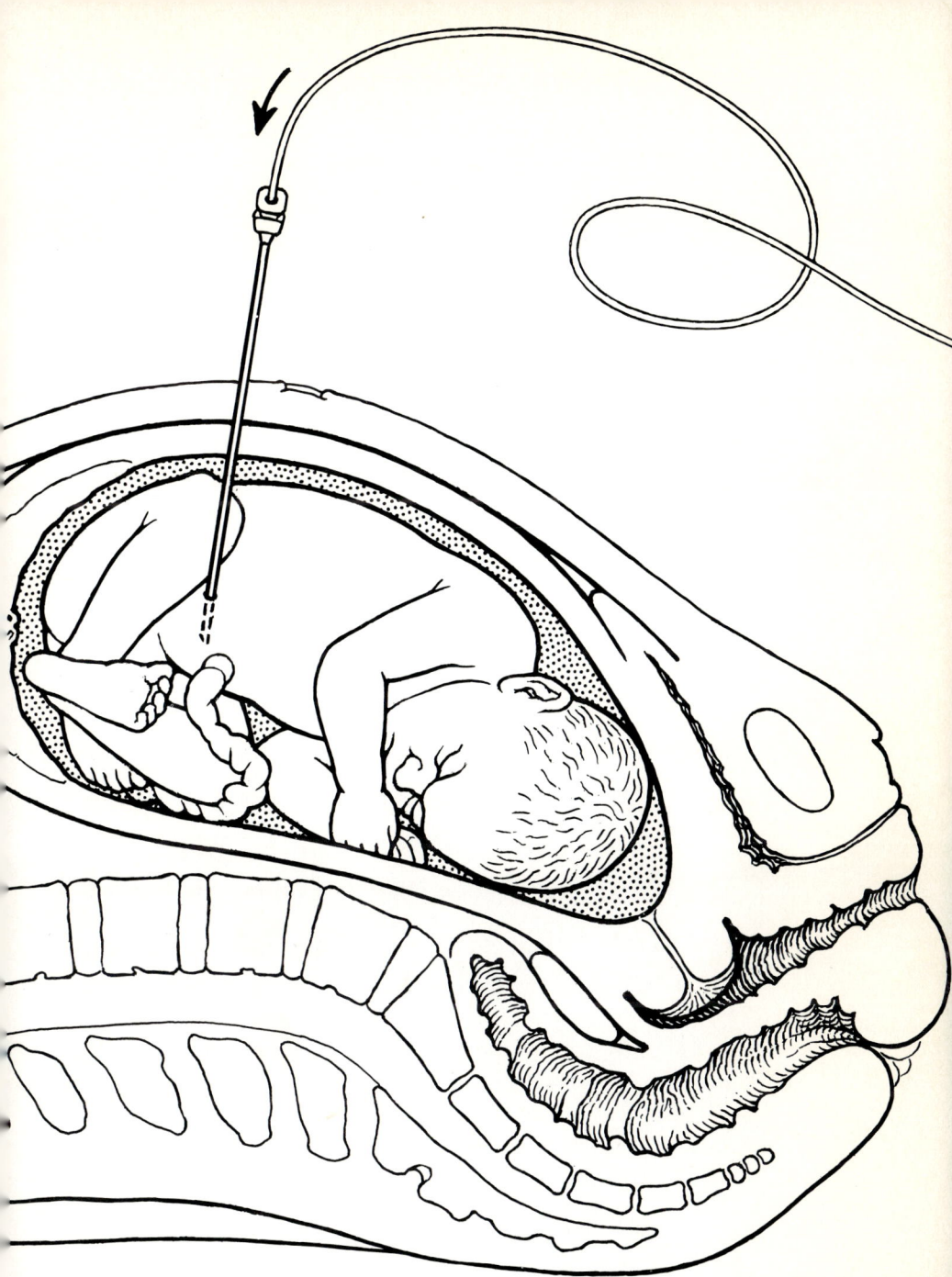

INTRAUTERINE TRANSFUSION. This diagram demonstrates how Rh-negative blood is injected into the unborn child by means of a needle that passes through the mother's abdominal cavity, the uterine wall, and into the baby's abdominal cavity. The Rh-negative blood is then absorbed into the baby's circulation. (From: Queenan, J.T. Amniocentesis and Transamniotic Fetal Transfusion for Rh Disease. CLINICAL OBSTETRICS AND GYNECOLOGY, 9: 491, 1966; Copyright © by Hoeber Medical Division of Harper & Row, Publishers, Incorporated.)

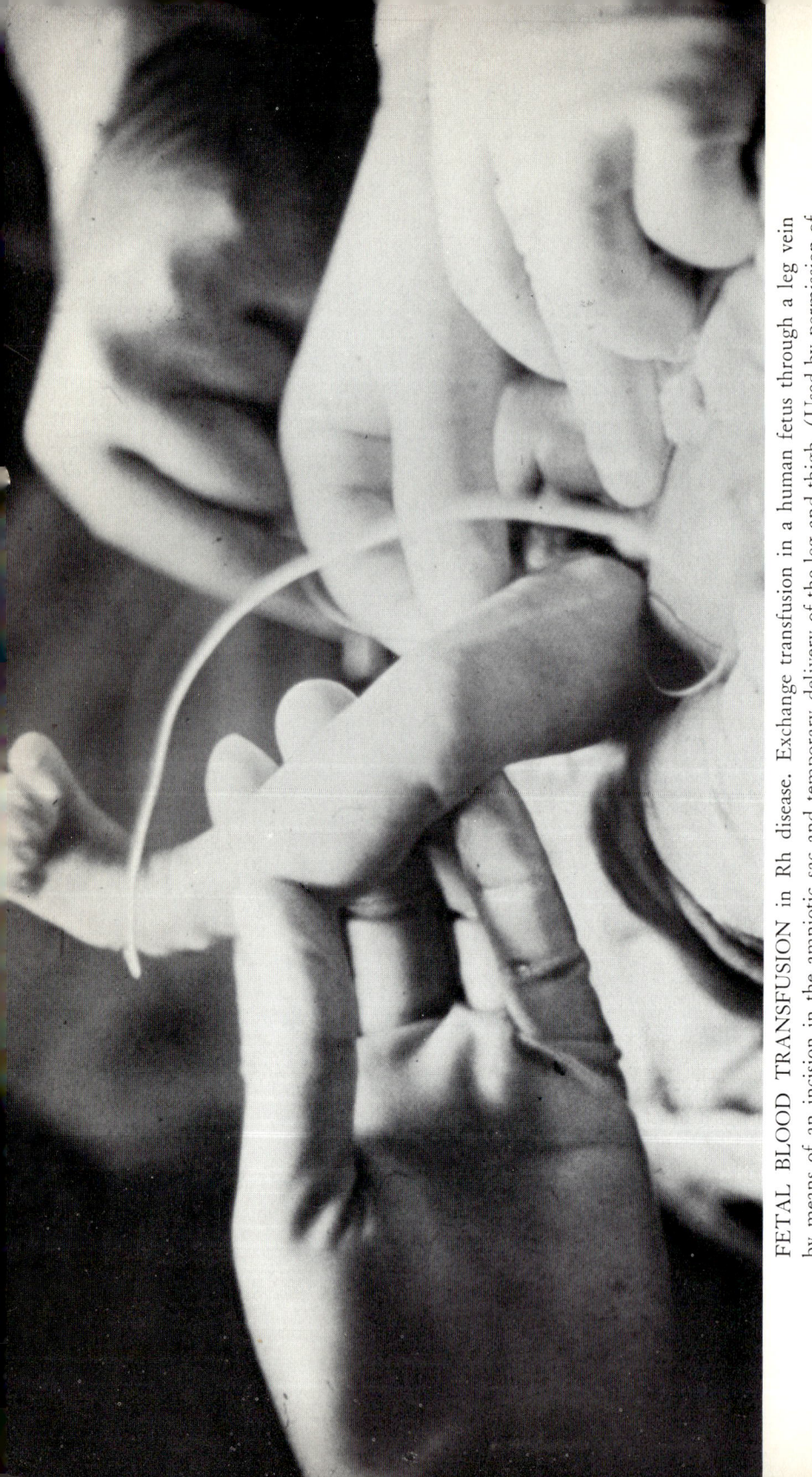

FETAL BLOOD TRANSFUSION in Rh disease. Exchange transfusion in a human fetus through a leg vein by means of an incision in the amniotic sac and temporary delivery of the leg and thigh. (Used by permission of MEDICAL WORLD NEWS and of Stanley H. Asensio, M.D., and associates, Department of Obstetrics and Gynecology, University of Puerto Rico Medical School.)

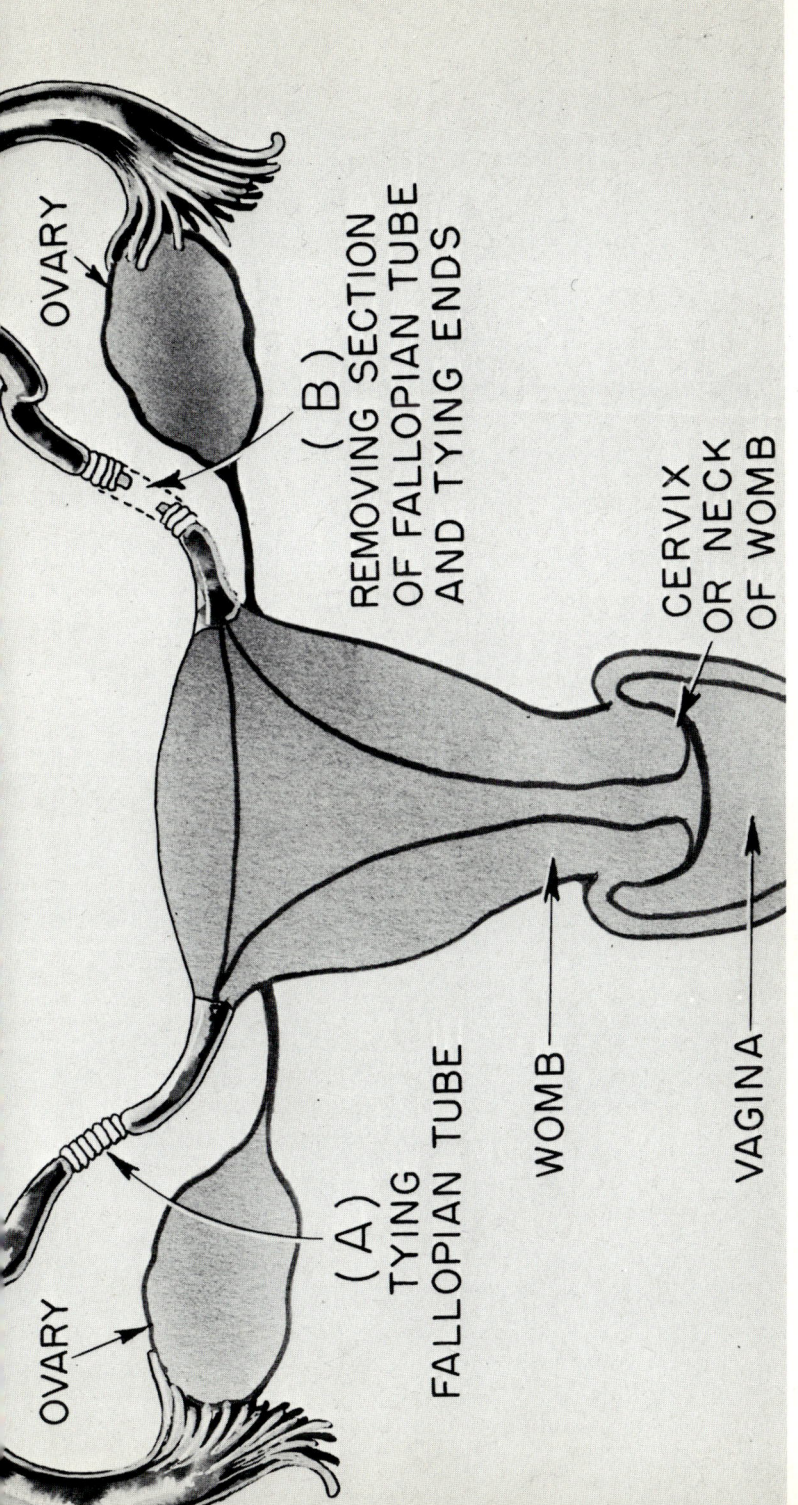

FEMALE STERILIZATION is performed by tying, or cutting and tying, the fallopian tubes. This prevents conception by blocking the passageway for the ovum, or egg, and preventing its union with the sperm. The ovum is eventually broken down and absorbed by the body. (Copyright © by Sexology Corp. Used by permission of SEXOLOGY magazine.)

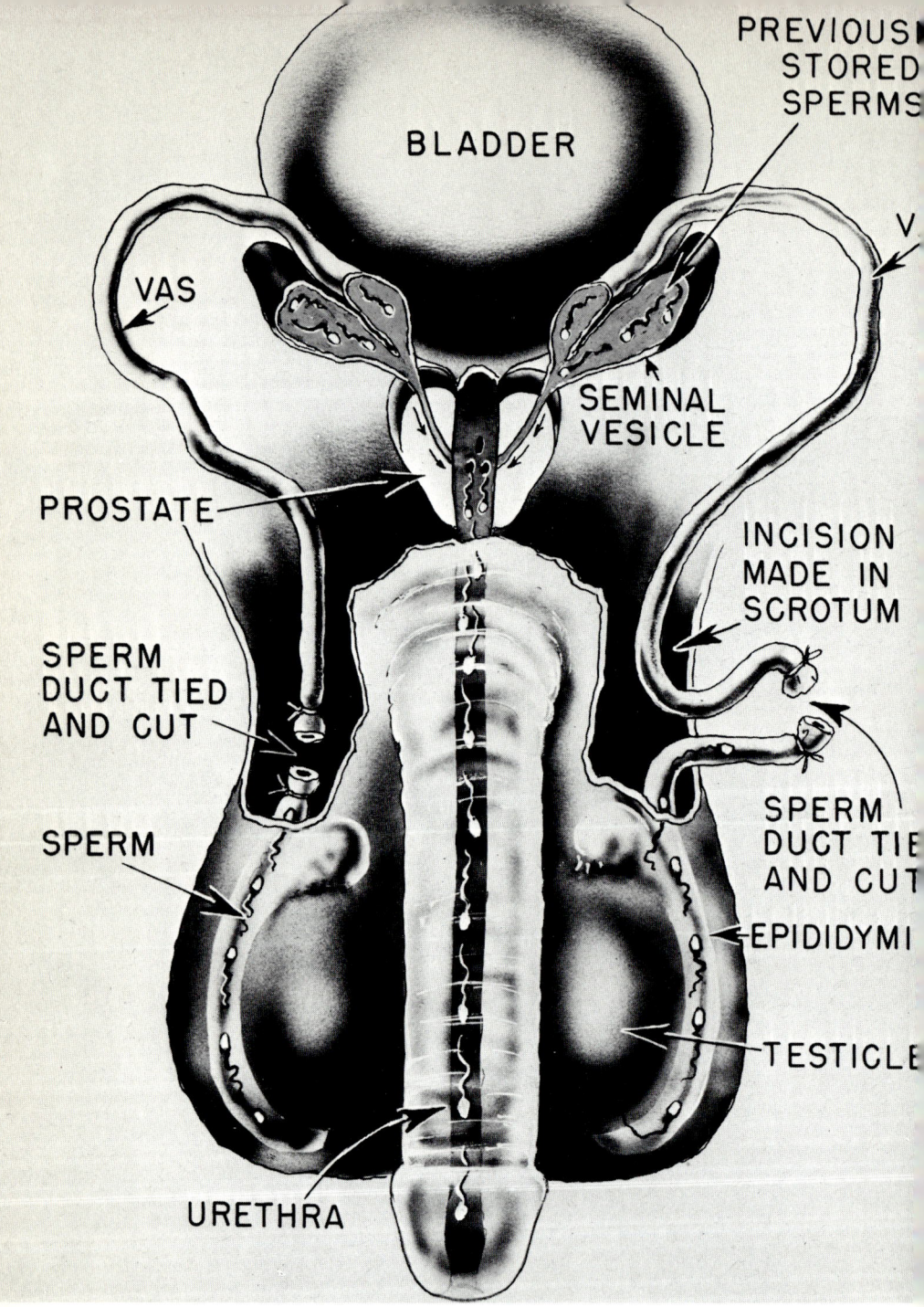

MALE STERILIZATION, or vasectomy, is a simple surgical procedure which takes less than half an hour and can be done in a doctor's office. An incision is made on each side of the scrotum, the sperm duct is cut and tied, and the ends are then returned to the scrotum, which is then closed. (Copyright © by Sexology Corp. Used by permission of SEXOLOGY magazine.)

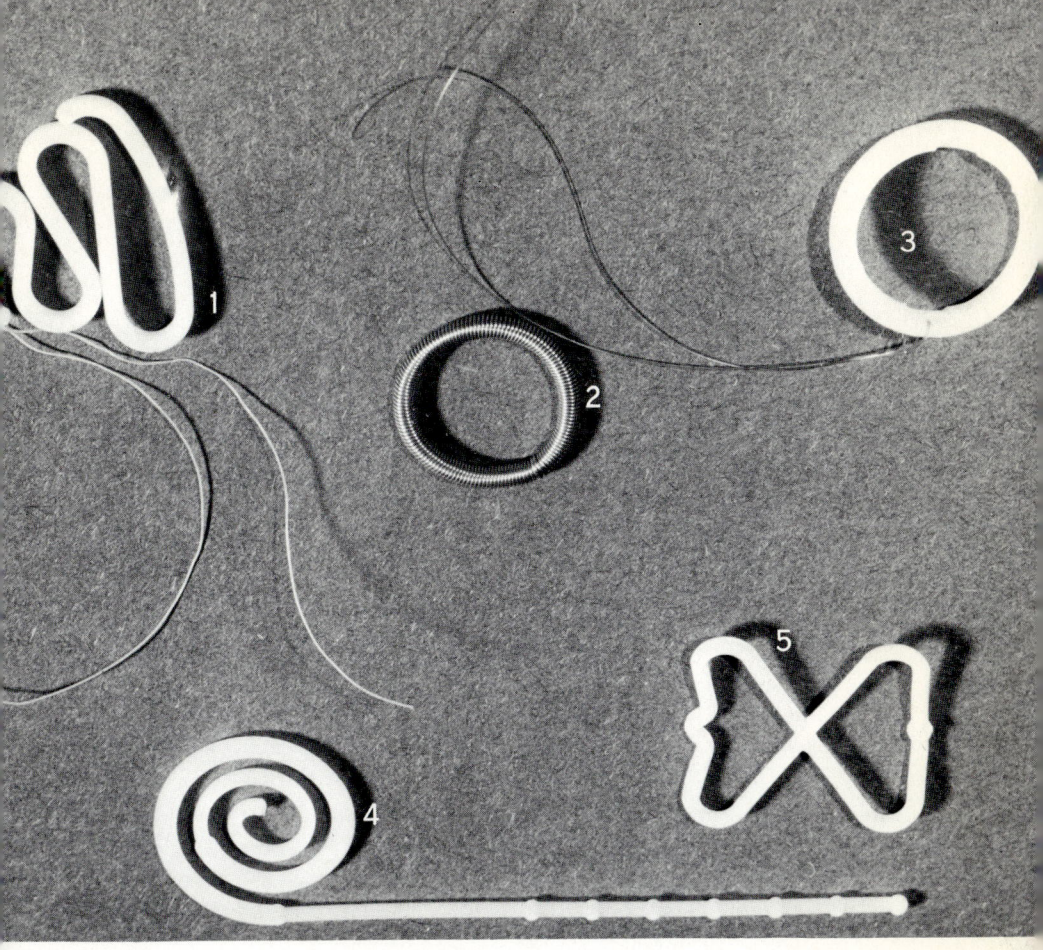

INTRAUTERINE DEVICES (IUD) act as foreign bodies in the uterus and prevent conception supposedly by increasing the normal speed of the ovum as it travels through the fallopian tube. Most devices are made of plastic; a few are made of stainless steel. Nylon threads are attached to some IUDs as a means for self-examination, or removal. Pictured above are examples of commonly used intrauterine devices: 1) Lippes loop; 2) Hall-Stone ring; 3) H. J. Davis ring (Johns Hopkins); 4) Margulies spiral, and 5) Birnberg bow. (Used by permission of CURRENT MEDICAL DIGEST, 32: 776, 1965; The Williams & Wilkins Company.)

NORMALLY AND ABNORMALLY SHAPED SPERM HEADS are shown in diagrammatic form. Abnormality in size or shape of the heads of spermatozoa is considered to be a possible cause of infertility in men. (From: MacLeod, J. A Possible Factor in the Etiology of Human Male Infertility. FERTILITY AND STERILITY, 13:29, 1962; Copyright © by Hoeber Medical Division of Harper & Row, Publishers, Incorporated.)

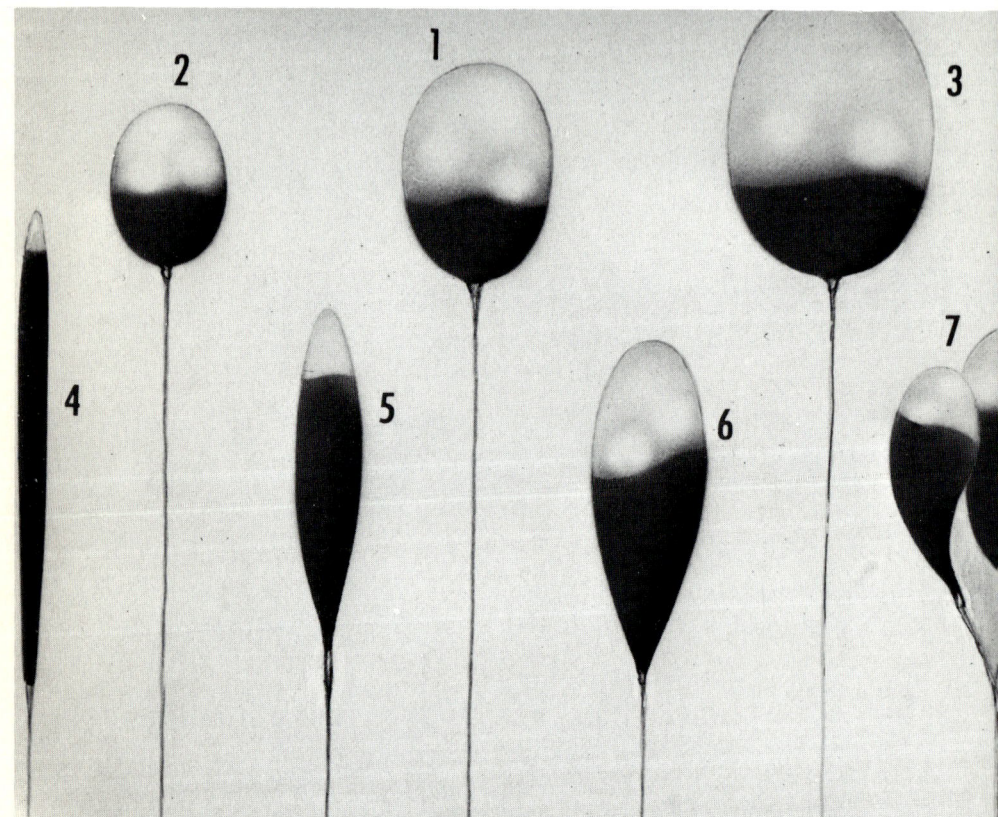

1) Normal size and head-shape; 2) normal head-shape, small size; 3) normal head-shape, large size; 4) acutely tapering head-shape ("stress cell"); 5) mildly-tapered head; 6) tendency toward tapering; and 7) bicephalic (two-headed).

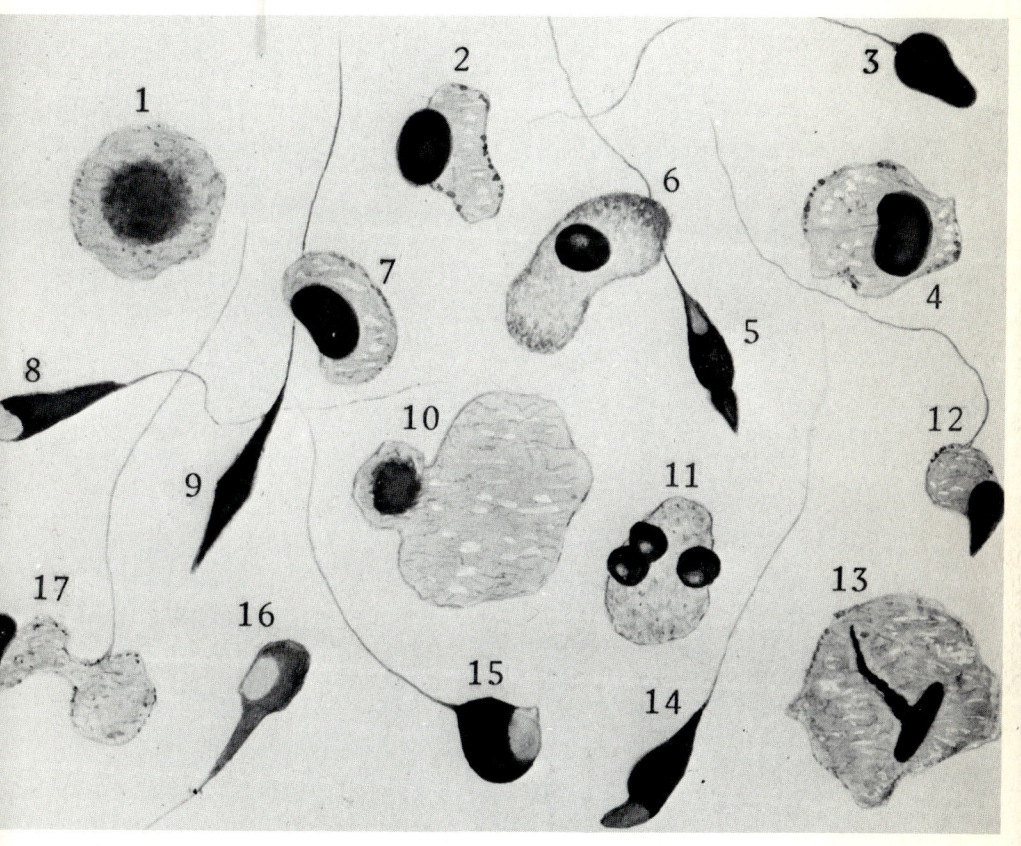

1) Degenerating immature form; 2) immature form (spermatid); 3) mature, amorphous (shapeless) spermatozoon; 4) immature form (spermatid); 5) mature cell, but tapering and amorphous head; 6) and 7) immature forms (spermatids); 8) and 9) amorphous and tapering forms; 10) degenerating spermatid; 11) multi-nucleated immature form (spermatid nuclei); 12) amorphous mature form; 13) immature form with distorted nuclear substance; and 14) through 17) mature but amorphous.

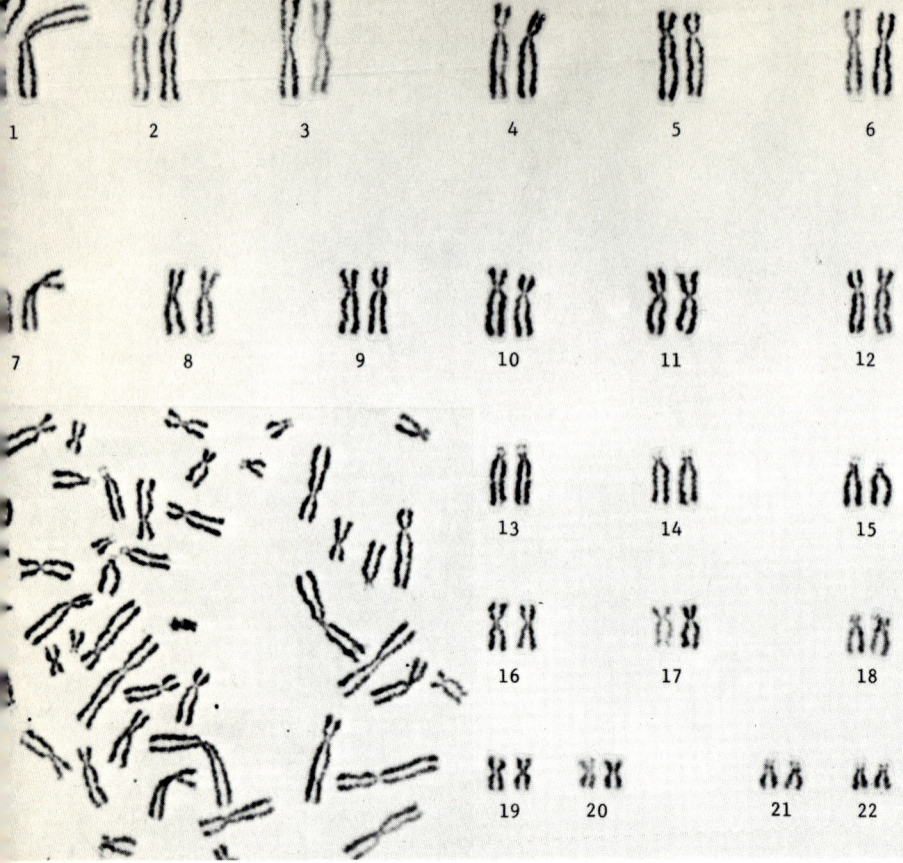

THE 46 CHROMOSOMES OF A NORMAL HUMAN MALE (XY). The lower left-hand insert shows the chromosomes as they appear under the microscope. The larger picture shows the chromosomes after their photographic images have been cut out and the pairs matched and arranged according to a standard classification. (Courtesy of James L. German, III, M.D., The New York Blood Center, New York.)

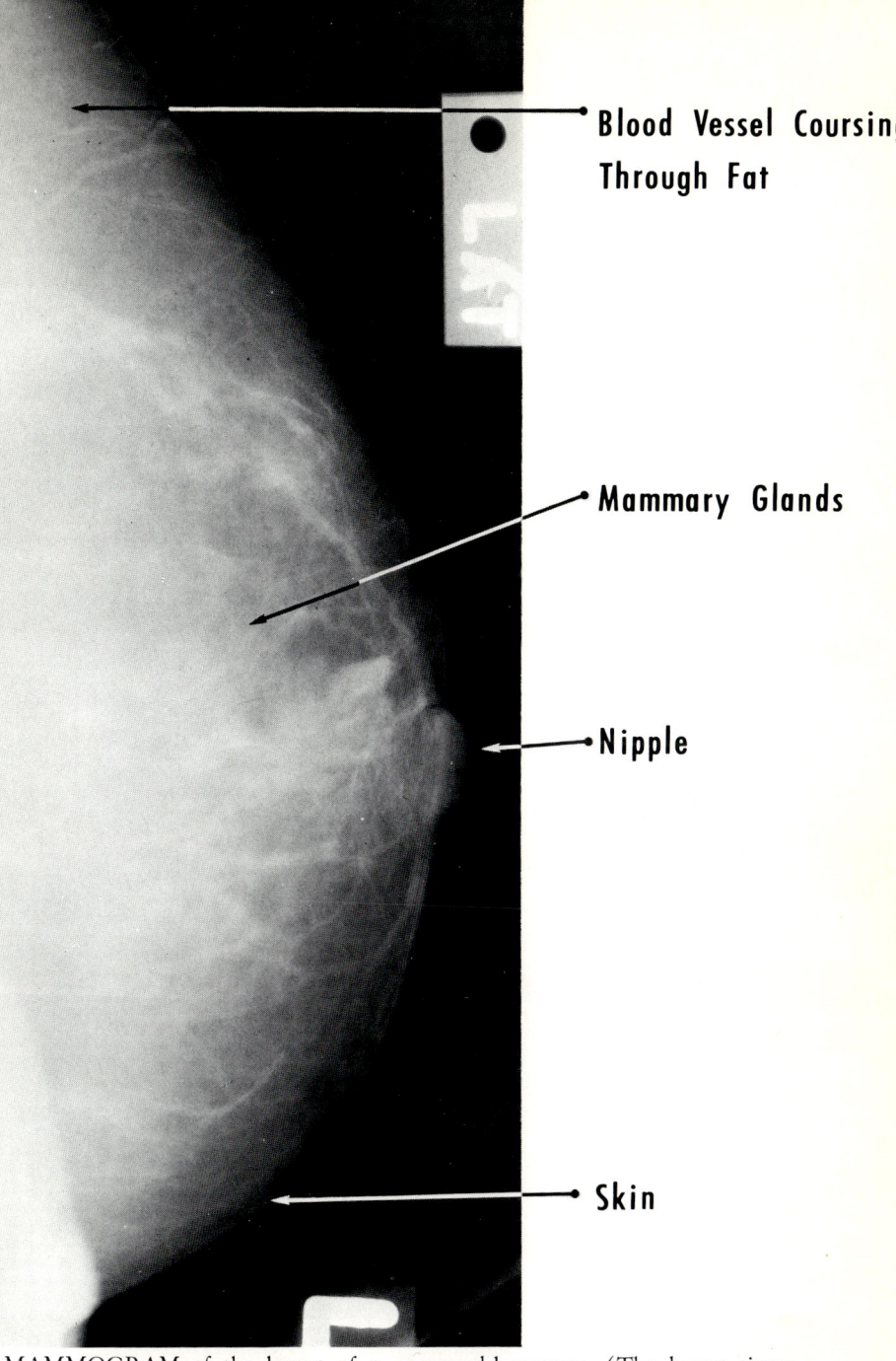

MAMMOGRAM of the breast of a 40-year-old woman. (The breast tissue is less dense at this age than in a younger woman.) This type of X-ray examination of the female breast can detect a growth too small to be felt by a physician. (Courtesy Norman Simon, M.D.)

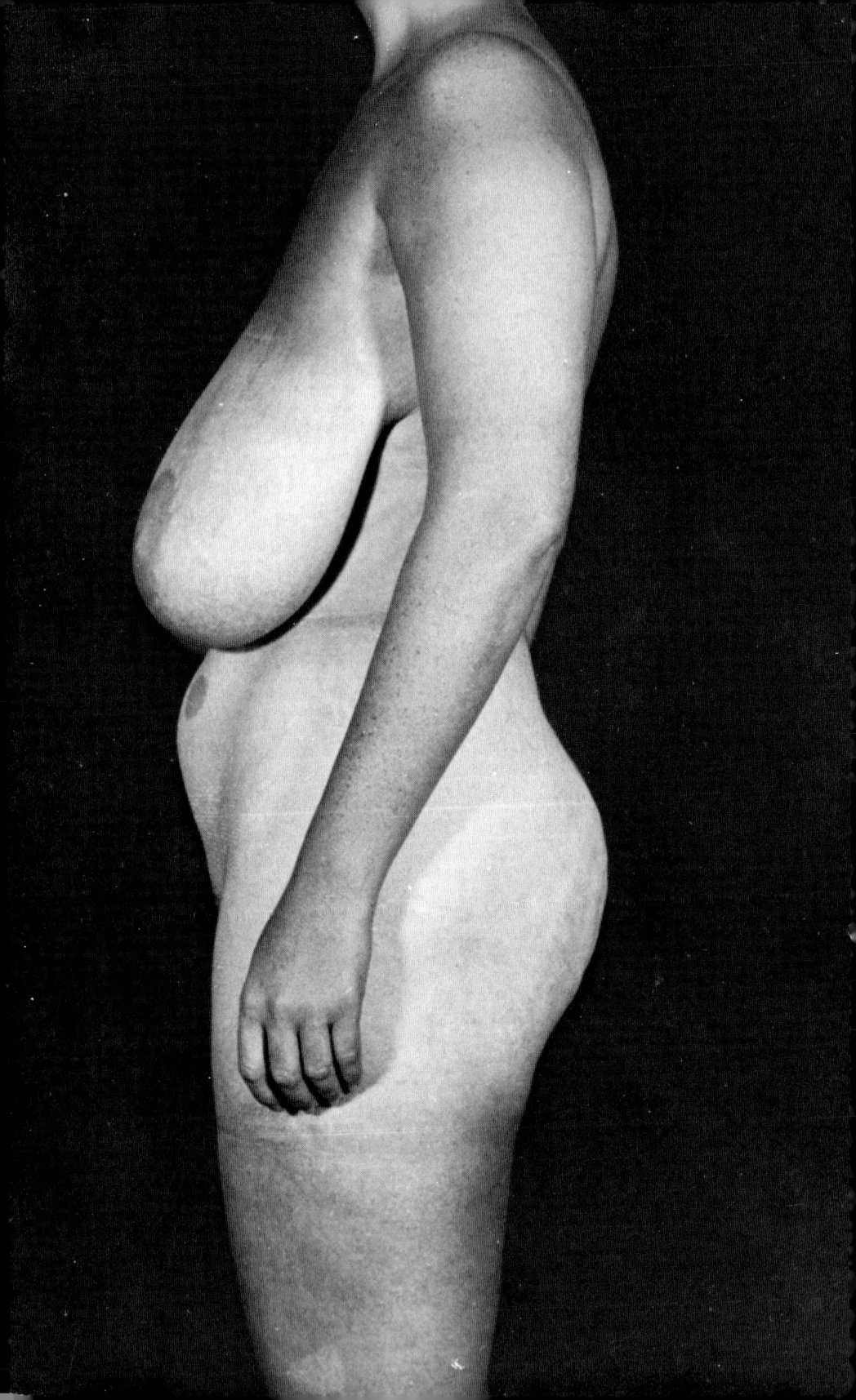

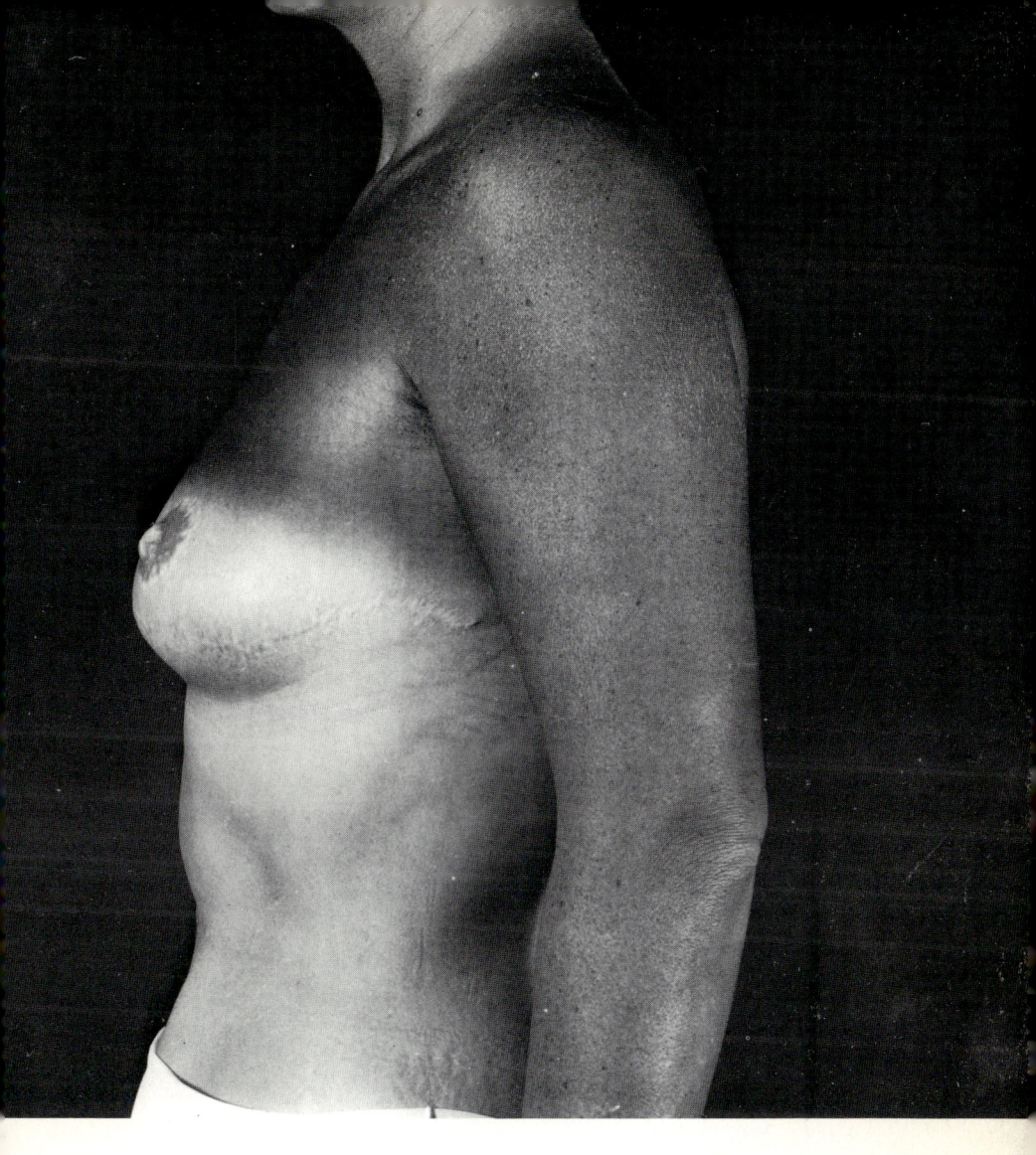

Before and after REDUCTION MAMMAPLASTY performed on a 32-year-old woman. (Courtesy Herbert Conway, M.D.)

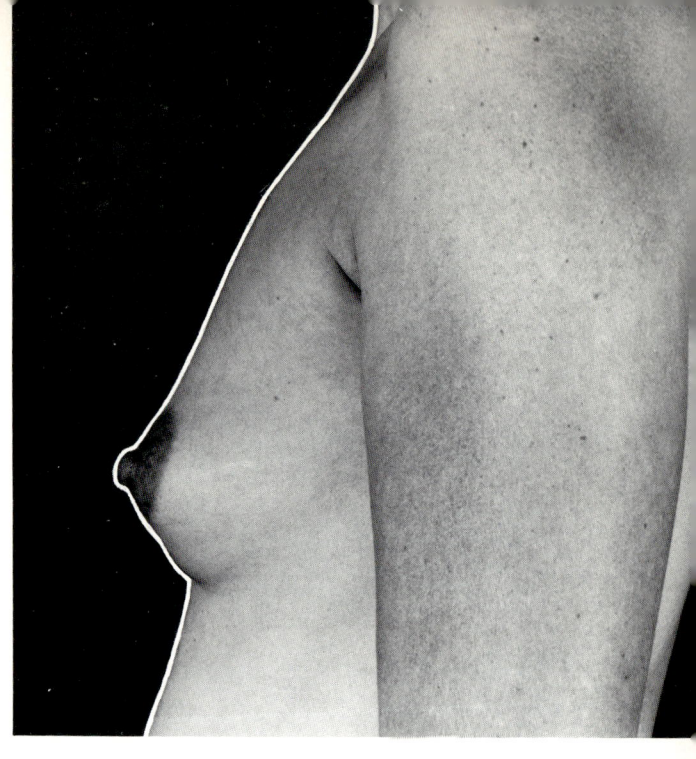

Before and after AUGMENTATION MAMMAPLASTY performed on a 36-year-old woman. (Courtesy Herbert Conway, M.D.)

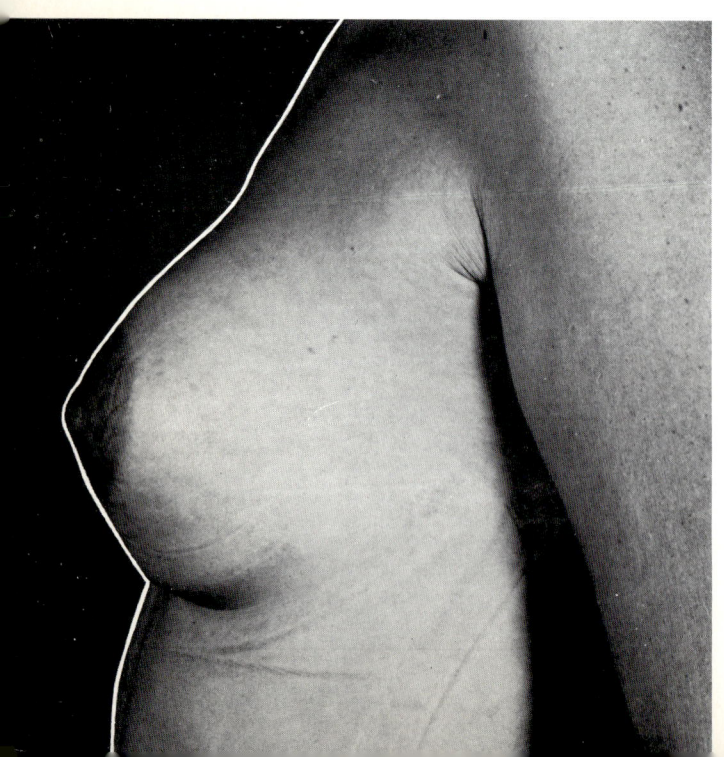

States, is associated with a number of known factors, among them: multiple births; toxemia; maternal diseases such as diabetes, high blood pressure, severe infections, and thyroid dysfunction; abnormal birth presentations; malformations of the uterus or incompetency of the cervix. The incidence of prematurity is higher in lower socioeconomic groups, and in mothers under the age of twenty and over forty. Recent studies point to a definite relationship between smoking in pregnancy and low birth weight infants, as well as to smoking in pregnancy and stillbirths. The premature baby has many disadvantages in coping with independent existence, and the more immature he is, the greater his handicaps.

The characteristics of a low birth weight or premature infant may be apparent both in subtle anatomical differences and in physiological functioning. The mechanisms regulating breathing are not fully developed; the nasal airway is narrow and easily obstructed; the blood pressure is low; heat regulation is faulty; the cough reflex is inadequate; the mechanism of swallowing is poorly developed in the smallest prematures, but even the less immature have feeding difficulty due to the shape, size, and lack of muscle development of the mouth and tongue; the small capacity of the stomach leads to regurgitation and vomiting; many metabolic (enzyme) systems for handling energy do not function properly. Probably the most tragic characteristic of low birth weight infants and prematures is their vulnerability to brain damage.

Today special attention is given during labor to mothers suspected of having a premature infant or those admitted to a hospital before the baby's due date. Drugs that might depress the infant's breathing are withheld and any other medications for the mother are kept to an absolute minimum. Formerly, it was believed that a premature infant benefited from delaying the tying of the cord, thereby giving the baby a placental blood transfusion. Recent studies have shown it is safer for the infant to have the cord clamped immediately following delivery, a practice now in common use.

Concerted efforts to further lower infant mortality and to

prevent those causes of mental retardation attributed to certain disorders occurring immediately after birth have led to new emphasis on special care in those critical early hours of life. Since 1960, when the Yale–New Haven Medical Center began to establish its Newborn Special Care Unit, about a dozen university-affiliated hospitals throughout the United States have since set up special intensive care units for sick and high-risk newborns. Upon delivery, when a baby's Apgar score shows he is in danger, the infant is rushed from the delivery room to the emergency nursery. There he is placed in a new type of incubator with an attached respirator and given oxygen. He is also given antibiotics for possible infection, glucose and water for energy, and put through a series of diagnostic tests. The baby is simultaneously prepared for transfusions, surgery, or whatever lifesaving or mind-saving procedure is indicated.

The unit at Yale–New Haven has, in its first seven years, succeeded in reducing its infant mortality rate to less than half of the national average. The other large medical centers with intensive care units for newborns are expected to report similar success. Smaller hospitals are now in the process of adapting similar types of units.

THE RESPIRATORY DISTRESS SYNDROME

One of the major causes of death during the first week of life is the respiratory distress syndrome. While it does not have an exact definition, this term is used to describe a group of characteristic symptoms found most frequently in premature infants, in babies born to diabetic mothers, and occasionally in infants delivered by caesarean section. It can also occur when a pregnancy is complicated by toxemia or hemorrhage before delivery. Full-size babies delivered vaginally rarely develop the condition.

The symptoms of the respiratory distress syndrome either directly follow a period of difficulty in establishing breathing at birth, or begin after an interval of a few hours. In addition to breathing difficulties, affected infants usually develop such problems as cyanosis (turning blue) from lack of oxygen, excessive fluid in the tissues, and metabolic acidosis.

There are a number of conditions included in the category of the respiratory distress syndrome, and each condition has its own mortality rate. One of these disorders is hyaline membrane disease, which took the life of Jacqueline Kennedy's infant Patrick. In hyaline membrane disease, currently the most common single cause of death among newborns, the infant's lungs cannot be properly expanded. A sticky material coats the lining membranes of the lungs, impeding the vital transport of oxygen from the air to the bloodstream.

Of the infants who die from hyaline membrane disease, about seventy-five percent succumb within the first forty-eight to sixty hours of life. Therefore, recent medical treatment has been geared to helping such an afflicted premature infant maintain life for two or three days, at which time a normal surface lining layer will begin to form in the lungs and the baby will start to show improvement.

Other causes of the respiratory distress syndrome are lung hemorrhage, pneumonia, and various degrees of lung collapse. Whatever the cause, the modern treatment of an affected infant may include a combination of the following: oxygen to nourish the brain and eliminate cyanosis, humidity in the incubator or by atomizer to loosen secretions, antibiotics to combat bacterial infections, and alkali therapy (concentrated sodium bicarbonate in glucose solution or a new buffering agent THAM) to correct metabolic acidosis.

Once an infant with the respiratory distress syndrome survives the first crucial days, there is little likelihood of its having any resultant lung impairment.

MINISURGERY

Every year in the United States more than half a million infants (one in sixteen of all live births) are born with some type of congenital malformation, ranging from clubfoot and cleft lip to defects in the development of the heart, circulatory system, nervous system, and gastrointestinal tract. Many such birth defects are being corrected today by a remarkable new type of surgical specialty—minisurgery, operating on the newborn. This "surgery in miniature," frequently completed within hours after birth, is saving the lives of tens of thousands of infants who, without minisurgery, would be certain to die. There have been successful operations even within an hour after birth on premature infants weighing little over one pound.

Because the patient and all his organs and body structures are so tiny, all minisurgical equipment is scaled down to doll-like proportions. There are anaesthesia masks barely bigger than a telephone mouthpiece, blood pressure machines with cuffs one inch wide and three inches long, heart-lung machines for open-heart surgery whose parts measure one-sixth of the size of similar devices used for adults. Surgical gloves are used as hot water bottles, as they are pliable and fit the contours of infants. Surgical instruments and test tubes are similarly miniaturized.

X-ray techniques and anaesthesia have been especially adapted and perfected for infant surgery. In 1967 a body-cooling technique used in adult open-heart surgery was reported to have been successfully applied in infant open-heart surgery. The cooling process protects the infant's brain during the time the heart is stopped and opened for repair. Another device adapted from adult use for infants undergoing open-heart surgery is the high pressure, or hyperbaric, chamber, in which the entire operation is performed. The high pressure of oxygen within the chamber forces extra oxygen into the patient's bloodstream and tissues, thereby nourishing his brain.

Despite their small size and apparent fragility, newborn infants have been found to withstand surgery surprisingly well and to recover often with dramatic speed. Of the approximately 40,000 babies born every year in the United States with heart defects, eighty percent are now being surgically cured. The success rate for operations on intestinal obstruction in the newborn is now ninety percent. Surgical correction of these and many other congenital defects offers an increasing number of newborn children today the possibility of living a virtually normal adult life.

FETAL SURGERY

The new science of fetal medicine has made remarkable discoveries in the heretofore mysterious and invisible world of the fetus. In learning about the anatomy, physiology, and environment of the fetus, physicians have been able to achieve diagnostic accuracy and to carry out intricate and startling treatments such as intrauterine transfusion in cases of Rh incompatibility. Such a procedure would have seemed impossible a few years ago, but now is becoming an established technique of modern obstetrics. A still more complete understanding of the intrauterine world may lead to another innovation in fetal medicine—fetal surgery, operations on the fetus even more delicate than those performed in minisurgery.

Successful experimental operations performed on animal fetuses in the past several years are setting the stage for intrauterine surgery on human fetuses to correct otherwise fatal or crippling birth defects. Before the turn of the century there were experiments on sheep in which the fetal lamb was removed from its mother's uterus and certain procedures performed. Many decades later came long-term experiments in which the fetal lamb was removed from the uterus and then replaced into the uterus, together with catheters, electrodes, and electronic transmitters—without the pregnancy being interrupted. This approach has subsequently been applied to other species, including rodents, dogs, and primates.

At the Oregon Regional Primate Research Center in Beaverton, Oregon, a few years ago a pregnant Rhesus monkey was placed under anaesthesia and her fetus was removed. After forty-five minutes of testing on the operating table, the monkey fetus was put back in the uterus, which was then sewn up. This mother monkey was able to continue her pregnancy and the baby monkey had a normal birth.

As techniques improve in diagnosing fetal abnormalities, human fetuses may be removed from their mothers' wombs for the administration of transfusions and medications as well as for correction of defects. The unborn child, the newest type of medical patient, seems destined to receive direct surgical care in the not too distant future.

21

The Problem of Mental Retardation

Since man's earliest eras, he has had to deal with those individuals who were mentally defective or incompetent. In some cultures these unfortunates were persecuted, in some ignored, and in others destroyed. Hundreds of years passed before any humane attempts were made even to protect the mentally handicapped from starvation and physical suffering. It was not until the nineteenth century that a broader interpretation of the doctrine of the brotherhood of man and the first insights of modern sciences introduced systematic attempts to care for the mentally retarded.

The first famous effort to educate a defective child dates back to 1799. A French physician, Jean Itard, diligently applied himself to trying to teach twelve-year-old Victor, the "Wild Boy of Aveyron," who had been captured in the forests of Aveyron. Victor had been examined and labeled severely retarded by the renowned physician, Philippe Pinel (reformer in the treatment and care of the mentally ill). After five years of intense effort, emphasizing sense and motor training, Dr. Itard succeeded only in bringing about changes in the boy's behavior, but otherwise his experiment was a failure. Victor died at the age of forty without ever having learned to talk or to live independently in society. Dr. Itard's account of his experiment is considered a classic in its field, and some of his ideas on sensory training have been incorporated in many current programs for both normal and retarded children.

Another century passed before an organized effort was made to teach retarded children in the United States. In 1896, the first day classes for the retarded were established in Providence, Rhode Island. More than sixty years were still to pass before the President of the United States appointed a Panel on Mental Retardation, in 1961, to study the causes, means of prevention, and treatment of the large public health problem that mental retardation presents. In addition to efforts of the Federal Government, many organizations have joined the growing movement to meet the challenges of mental retardation—state governments, parents' groups, charitable groups, and private foundations. These groups are currently engaged in intensive efforts to utilize the latest advances in the fields of pediatrics, nursing, psychology, sociology, social work, education, and vocational training to bring new hope and a brighter future to all mentally retarded people.

DEFINING MENTAL RETARDATION

All infants at birth differ from one another in heredity, birth experience, appearance, temperament, intelligence, and potential. As there is a tremendous variation in the degree of intellectual capacity among so-called normal children, there is also a wide variation in the degree of mental retardation among the children who fall within the lowest range of intellectual capacity.

Mental retardation is felt to be due to arrested or incomplete development of the brain during prenatal life or early in childhood. Mental retardation is not to be confused with mental illness, although the two conditions may coexist in the same individual. Mental illness, even though it can occur in childhood, usually follows a period of relatively normal intellectual development, becoming apparent in adolescence or adult life.

While mentally retarded children are defined differently from the medical, legal, educational, psychosocial, and neuropsychological points of view, the great majority (an estimated 89.0 percent) on testing show an I.Q.—intelligence quotient —ranging from 53–75. These children are classified as *mildly* retarded, and despite limited ability to learn, can feed and dress themselves, have control of bowel and bladder functions, have adequate speech functions, and can read and write. With special classroom teaching, these children can acquire practical and academic skills equivalent to a third to sixth grade level. With proper training, they can achieve vocational and social skills sufficient to hold a simple job.

Moderately retarded children (I.Q. 36–52) and *severely* retarded children (I.Q. 20–35) represent 6.0 percent and 3.5 percent, respectively, of all retarded children. These two groups are considered trainable but need protective supervision. *Profoundly* retarded children (I.Q. 0–19) represent 1.5 percent and are generally considered untrainable. Although they may walk and have primitive speech development, they require complete custodial care and supervision.

CAUSES OF MENTAL RETARDATION

The known causes of mental retardation fall into four basic categories: 1) hereditary or genetic factors existing before or at the time of conception; 2) maternal diseases and complications arising during pregnancy; 3) birth injuries to the child; and 4) infectious diseases or injuries occurring after birth but before completion of mental development.

Low or subnormal intelligence may be transmitted as an

inherited characteristic from one or both parents in much the same way as genius is thought to be passed on from one generation to the next, or such physical characteristics as coloring and body build. Certain defects of metabolism genetically transmitted are also responsible for retarded brain function. Two of the most well-known examples of such conditions are phenylketonuria (PKU) and galactosemia, these names being derived from chemical substances found in excess in these conditions.

During pregnancy, certain diseases in the mother can have an adverse effect on the fetal brain and its subsequent development—rubella is perhaps the best known example. Complications of pregnacy such as toxemia, uterine hemorrhage, and Rh incompatibility between mother and child—and prematurity—are other possible causes of mental retardation.

Authorities have estimated that not more than one to two percent of mental retardation is due to cerebral injuries connected with the birth process. Included in this category are prolonged or difficult labor, premature separation of the placenta, compression of the umbilical cord, and difficult breech or transverse presentations.

Diseases during early childhood which produce inflammation of the central nervous system, or head injuries during infancy, can cause mental retardation. Meningitis, invariably fatal until the past generation, now responds to antibiotics and new techniques of medical care. However, this disease today is responsible for approximately one percent of mentally retarded people who are institutionalized.

Altogether, there are more than a hundred known causes of mental retardation. But these probably account for no more than twenty-five percent of all the mentally retarded. The remaining seventy-five percent are retarded for reasons unknown to date. Most of these are mildly retarded; their low level of intelligence is often not recognized until their learning difficulties become apparent to parents or teachers. Because mild retardation is more frequently found among children of low socioeconomic background, poor diet, inadequate prenatal and infant care, or even a lack of mental stimulation in early childhood may be totally or partially responsible. In contrast, the more serious forms of retardation, while rare, seem to show no social class predilection.

NEW DISCOVERIES IN METABOLIC DISORDERS

There are many rare inborn errors of metabolism, some of which lead to mental retardation. Probably the most publicized in recent years is *phenylketonuria*—PKU—which is said to account for about one percent of older retardates in institutions. Inherited by a single recessive gene, PKU affects about one in 10,000 to 20,000 newborns. It causes the infant to be incapable of forming an important amino acid, tyrosine, from phenylalanine—a substance present in most foods, including milk. Before birth, the placental circulation removes excessive phenylalanine. After birth, however, phenylalanine accumulates in the blood, its level rising continually as the newborn infant ingests milk. The high blood levels of certain metabolic products of phenylalanine produce progressive brain impairment.

Fortunately, PKU may be diagnosed by means of a blood test or a urine test shortly after a baby is born. The blood test is done while the child is still in the hospital nursery and is then repeated in four weeks. The urine test, while simpler to perform, cannot be done until the infant is three weeks old and is repeated at six weeks of age. A small strip of chemically treated absorbent paper or "test tape," (like that used in many urine tests) placed on a freshly wet diaper or in a urine specimen will change color if PKU is present. Because earlier diagnosis can be achieved by means of a blood test, a routine screening test for PKU using a spot of blood on filter paper is coming into use.

The treatment of PKU is a diet consisting mainly of a mixture of nutritive substances containing only a minimally essential amount of phenylalanine. The earlier in life the dietary treatment is begun, the better the results. A number of states now support massive screening programs to test newborn infants for PKU. In New York, for example, statewide screening tests for PKU begun in 1965 have led to the discovery of more than eighty children with this condition. By early diagnosis and treatment, mental retardation and other behavioral symptoms of brain damage in PKU can be greatly lessened or perhaps prevented entirely.

Healthy people with a family history of PKU or mental retardation can now be tested to find out whether or not they are carriers of the PKU gene.

Another recessively inherited metabolic disorder that can lead to various degrees of mental retardation is *galactosemia*. Less common than PKU, galactosemia is estimated to affect one child in each 30,000 to 40,000 live births. In this condition, galactose—a carbohydrate constituent in milk—accumulates in the blood because of the absence of the enzyme needed to convert it into glucose. Galactosemia develops as the infant begins to take in milk; it can result in vomiting, diarrhea, jaundice, mental retardation, and even death.

Diagnosis of galactosemia can now be made by means of urine or blood tests as simple as those for PKU. Treatment consists of giving the affected infant a special low lactose milk substitute and maintaining a very low lactose diet throughout early childhood. Galactose tolerance may improve as the child grows older, and then the diet may be modified. In the past year or two, several states have begun pilot programs of screening tests for galactosemia in newborns which may become statewide like the test for PKU. In addition, there is a method (similar to that used in PKU) of diagnosing healthy carriers of the galactosemia gene.

Other metabolic disturbances associated with mental retardation for which there are now methods of diagnosis and treatment are: Hartnup syndrome, a condition similar to PKU but with a characteristic rash; Wilson's disease, a disorder in which copper is deposited in the tissues of the brain, liver, and other organs; and maple-syrup urine disease, named for the characteristic odor emitted by the urine of affected individuals. It is likely that other potential genetic defects in metabolism associated with mental retardation will be discovered. Hopefully, these too may be prevented or moderated by long-term dietary adjustment or medication.

PART VI

THE INFERTILE COUPLE

22

Sterility and Fertility

It is difficult for the woman who has conceived easily and produced the number of children she planned to imagine the plight of the woman who is involuntarily childless. A woman who desperately wants children and cannot bear them is willing to undergo any kind of test, treatment, or operation to reverse her barren state.

Problems of sterility and infertility have concerned mankind from ancient times, when primitive peoples invoked water nymphs and tree spirits to make them fertile. Rolling on the ground under a lone apple tree was considered helpful in obtaining offspring. Some societies employed imitative magic, as did Indian women of Peru who wrapped up stones like babies and left them at the foot of larger stones. Other cultures relied on insect and animal charms—an Indian tribe of Vancouver Island believed a decoction of wasps' nests or flies taken internally would make barren women as prolific as insects. Fertility rites were vital parts of all primitive religions.

Man's timeless quest for blessed fertility has presented a challenge to medicine men, priests, and physicians throughout history. Hippocrates is credited with devising the following diagnostic test for infertility: "If a woman has not conceived and you wish to determine whether conception be possible, wrap her up in a cloak underneath which incense should be burned. If the odour seems to pass through the body to the nose and mouth, then she is not sterile." It was also the observation of Hippocrates that: "As a good proof of the sort of physical characteristics which are favourable to conception, consider the case of serving wenches. No sooner do they have intercourse with a man than they become pregnant, on account of their sturdy physique and their leanness of flesh."

Procreation has been considered an essential aspect of marriage in almost every society, and women have always been assigned the blame for barren unions. Even in many monogamous societies the husband of a childless woman was allowed to take a second wife or a concubine, or else he was allowed to dissolve his marriage if his wife did not conceive.

Now, after thousands of years of shouldering the full responsibility for infertility, women are being told—on the basis of much new medical evidence—that their husbands are just as likely to be responsible for a "barren marriage" (*sterilitas matrimonii*) as themselves. In the past two decades the expanding knowledge of the physiology of human semen has brought a new understanding of male sterility. Much of this knowledge stems from the increasing use by veterinarians of the centuries-old practice of artificial insemination employed in animal husbandry.

Before 1958, women who did not ovulate stood little chance of conceiving despite the many medications and treatments that were given. Since that time, the fundamental mechanisms of ovulation have come under direct control of drugs that induce ovulation. One of these, paradoxically, was found in the search for drugs that would *inhibit* ovulation—precursors of The Pill.

In the United States one husband and wife among every ten

come to marriage incapable of initiating pregnancy. Another ten percent of couples are frustrated in their reproductive efforts by repeated abortion. Thus, inability to reproduce affects an estimated 3,500,000 American couples. Up until recently, about thirty-five percent of couples with long-established fertility problems have achieved pregnancy after thorough medical diagnosis and treatment. As more is known about reproductive physiology, the chance of success for the infertile couple should be even greater.

THE NEW TERMINOLOGY

In current usage, *sterility* is the term applied when an individual has some irreversible factor preventing procreation. *Infertility* denotes the inability of a married couple to initiate a pregnancy. Infertility is considered *primary* and *absolute* when conception has never occurred, and is called *secondary* and *relative* when at least one pregnancy is followed by one year of involuntary barrenness.

The fertility of the biological entity represented by a married couple depends upon the combination of individual fertilities. Marital fertility refers to a couple's combined capacity for reproduction; it does not necessarily mean that both partners have a good fertility—one may have low fertility and the other may compensate by having high fertility. On the other hand, infertile or barren marriage may result from the union of two people of low fertility, each of whom might prove fertile with another marriage partner.

Among fertile couples, pregnancy is achieved in approximately fifty percent within a month after having regular intercourse without contraception. An estimated seventy-five percent are successful by the end of six months, and ninety percent by the end of one year.

THE INFLUENCE OF AGE

It is well known that a woman's age helps to determine her fertility, conception rate, and successful gestation, all of which start to decline after the age of twenty-five, and by age thirty-three, are considerably reduced.

If a wife is between the ages of eighteen and twenty-five, two years of involuntary infertility would warrant medical consultation. Between the ages of twenty-six and thirty-two, one year is sufficiently long to wait before seeking professional advice. Most fertility experts agree that if the wife is over thirty-two, no more than six months should be allowed to pass before she has her infertility investigated.

A husband's age by itself is not considered an important factor in an infertile marriage.

CAUSES OF MALE INFERTILITY

As many as four out of every ten infertile marriages may be primarily due to the husband. Investigation of the quality of the husband's sperm is usually undertaken early in the study of an infertile couple.

A complete and thorough history is taken from the husband—his previous illnesses (such as mumps); his occupational hazards (unprotected exposure to radioactive substances or X-rays, or to metals like lead, iron, copper, and zinc used in painting, printing, and plumbing, or exposure to excessive heat); and his social habits (such as excessive smoking and alcoholic consumption). The examining physician discusses with the husband such personal matters as premature ejaculation, use of precoital lubricants, frequency of intercourse, sexual drive and variations in potency, and positions used during intercourse.

There are four main factors that determine male infertility: 1) disturbances in spermatogenesis (due to endocrine insufficiency, disorders of the testicle, or varicocele—varicose veins within the scrotum); 2) obstruction of the sperm ducts (due to infections such as gonorrhea, the presence of cysts in the epididymis, traumatic and congenital causes); 3) changes in the seminal fluid (the quality and amount); and 4) abnormalities of ejaculation (due to structural, endocrinological, and psychological causes, certain kinds of prostate operations, diabetes, certain medications prescribed for other disorders, drug addiction, or syphilis).

CAUSES OF FEMALE INFERTILITY

While it is relatively easy to establish that a husband's sperm cannot fertilize his wife's ova, it is usually more difficult to determine the reasons for female infertility, as it may be caused by conditions anywhere in the body. Several months may be required to track down the one or more relevant factors.

A detailed medical history is taken from the wife, which is similar to that taken from her husband. In addition, the examining physician will want to know the woman's complete menstrual history: age at onset of menstruation, duration and frequency of flow, amount of bleeding, presence or absence of pain, any menstrual irregularities, and any periods of amenorrhea (no menstruation). The physician also discusses such personal matters as premarital and postmarital intercourse, and may inquire about the marriage partners' previous practices of contraception. The wife is asked to describe any condition that had required medical or surgical treatment. What the doctor learns from taking the wife's history gives valuable clues to possible causes of her infertility, especially if she has had certain pelvic infections, endometriosis (the presence in abnormal locations of cells that normally line the uterus), thyroid disturbance, or repeated early abortion.

Because female infertility can be due to disorders of the vulva, vagina, cervix, uterus, tubes, or ovaries, a detailed pelvic examination is performed. Such barriers to conception as unsuspected growths, endometriosis, narrowed cervical opening, or congenital malformations are disclosed by the examination.

The four major causes of female infertility, in descending order of frequency, are: 1) tubal factors (mechanical obstruction or disturbances of tubal contractility); 2) cervical factors (abnormal position of the cervix, narrowing of the cervical opening, changes in the quality and amount of cervical mucus); 3) endocrine factors (disorders of the thyroid, pituitary, or adrenal glands; disturbances in the hormones affecting the menstrual cycle; emotional problems affecting ovarian function); and 4) gross pelvic factors (malformations of the uterus ranging from "unicorn" uterus to double uterus, abnormal position of the uterus, certain fibroid tumors).

A NEW APPROACH TO UNEXPLAINED INFERTILITY

Although many diagnostic tests have been devised for both sexes over the past forty years, the cause of infertility in about fifteen percent of couples has yet to be explained. The 1960's have introduced a new theory that is currently being tested—the wife in some way is allergic to her husband's sperm cells and/or seminal fluid.

It has been known for years that in animals or humans an allergic or sensitization response can be induced by injecting foreign protein—even in minute amounts—at frequent intervals. When one considers how much and how often foreign protein is "injected" intravaginally during a couple's marital life, it would not be altogether surprising to discover that a woman could become allergic to her husband's sperm.

Substantiating evidence has been found in the study of four hundred women with a five-year or longer history of infertility. In the blood of fourteen percent of these women, antibodies to their husbands' spermatozoa were discovered. These antibodies were found to have been markedly reduced when repeated exposure to their husbands' sperm was prevented by the use of condoms or total sexual abstention for several months. It was then anticipated that pregnancy would occur at the time of ovulation following unprotected intercourse. About forty women followed this regimen, and after resumed unprotected intercourse, twenty-four became pregnant. Whether this was due to reduction of sensitivity to their husbands' sperm is not yet known.

In addition to bloodstream antibodies to spermatozoa, it is very possible that there may be tissue antibodies anywhere along the female reproductive tract that destroy or otherwise inactivate sperm. Intensive studies are being made to locate such antibodies, for if they are found to be present, there might be methods for inhibiting this antibody response.

In one experiment seventeen women in early pregnancy, all of whose last three (or more) pregnancies had ended in spontaneous abortion, were given grafts of their husbands' skin, as well as skin provided by non-husband donors. These women tended to reject the grafts of their husbands' skin more rapidly than the donor's skin. Surprisingly, about seventy-five percent of these particular "aborters" who had received the skin grafts went on to deliver at term. Whether the skin grafting was indeed therapeutic is still under investigation.

Other types of harmful hyperimmune response leading to infertility could be "autosensitization" to one's own ova or sperm cells, and even sensitivity in a woman to her own fetus or different groups of cells within the fetus—not merely the already proven instances of maternal-fetal Rh and ABO sensitivity.

In testing the theory of allergic infertility, much is to be learned which may be of direct benefit to the couple who want a child. Of the fifteen percent of couples whose infertility is unexplained by current diagnostic techniques, it is impossible at this time to predict how many will eventually be helped by future findings in the complex field of immune response.

23

Diagnosis and Treatment of Male Infertility

Male infertility is the inability of a man to produce healthy sperm and to deliver them for fertilization. It is not a reflection of a man's virility (in fact, excessive coitus is sometimes blamed for male infertility) but may be merely some impairment in spermatogenesis. The male factor in infertility is more easily diagnosed than any of the female factors; usually a detailed history and physical examination, with special attention given to the genitalia, and at least two examinations of semen are sufficient for recognition of a deficiency. If the semen analysis reveals certain abnormalities, a testicular biopsy is sometimes performed to rule out any systemic disease.

NORMAL TESTICULAR FUNCTION

The development of normal sexual anatomy, as well as function, depends upon an intensely complicated series of events beginning early in fetal life. The regularity with which the male infant is born with its reproductive glands—the testes or testicles—already outside its body in the scrotal sac is attested to by the very derivation of the word *testis* from the Latin, meaning *witness* (testifying to the maleness?). The arrival of the testes in the scrotum is the culmination of a long anatomical journey from their original position somewhat below the embryonic kidneys. A person whose testicles have failed to descend, though he may be male in every other respect, will be infertile because the high temperatures of intraabdominal existence inhibit sperm formation. If the testicles descend by themselves or are surgically brought down into the scrotum between the ages of four and six, their function will usually be preserved.

At the time of puberty, the pituitary gonadotrophic hormones stimulate the testes within the scrotal cavity to initiate their double function of producing sperm cells and manufacturing male sex hormones, mainly testosterone. In spite of the fact that each olive-shaped testicle measures only about $1\frac{1}{2}$ inches in length and weighs less than an ounce, they are the source of billions of cells from which spermatozoa are formed —about 100 million daily.

To reach their discharge as fertilizing agents, the sperm must travel through half a mile of highly convoluted tubing— passing from the testes via the epididymes (behind and above the testes) through spermatic ducts, seminal vesicles and ducts to ejaculatory ducts at the base of the prostate gland, through the erect penis, finally emerging from the urethral opening at the moment of orgasm.

The fertility of the human male lasts far longer than that of his female partner. Cell changes within the testicles that reduce fertility do not occur until a man is fifty-five or sixty years of age. Many men in their sixties and seventies have been known to initiate pregnancy.

EXAMINATION OF SEMEN

The discovery of swimming spermatozoa of dogs and other animals was first described in 1677 by Anton van Leeuwenhoek, the Dutch amateur scientist who became known as the father of microbiology. His observation of the motion of sperm across a microscopic field formed a basis for the long-held assumption that sperm reach their destination for fertilization by means of their own motility. Only recently have studies shown that the muscular contractions of the uterus and fallopian tubes may be as important as sperm movement for migration up through the female genital tract. Although sperm counts have been done in the study of male infertility for decades, in the last ten years great accuracy has been achieved in measuring the rate of progression of sperm.

Inadequate sperm (*oligospermia*) or absence of sperm (*azoospermia*) may be the sole cause of an infertile marriage. To determine whether conception is possible, a "screening examination" of the husband's semen is made from a specimen collected after at least three full days of abstinence from intercourse. The method of collection may vary with different individuals. The semen is frequently collected in a clean, dry, wide-mouthed glass jar either by masturbation or by coitus interruptus (withdrawal before orgasm). Rubber condoms are not used in the collection of semen because they are detrimental to sperm. For collecting semen specimens, there is, however, a sheathlike device made of polyethylene which has no effect on sperm motility. Also available is a plastic condom which is perforated to meet the moral principles of Catholic couples undergoing infertility diagnosis.

Within three hours after ejaculation, the semen specimen is examined for volume, number of spermatozoa (total sperm count in a cubic centimeter of ejaculate), the percentage of motile sperm in the specimen, and the proportion of sperm having normal morphologic features, or shapes. Such an analysis frequently discloses such disorders as: 1) inadequate numbers of sperm (less than 20 million per cubic centimeter) with poor motility and morphology; 2) adequate sperm count (20 to 150 million per cubic centimeter) with poor motility and morphology; 3) poor motility with adequate count and good morphology; and 4) low percent of active spermatozoa in specimens containing very high sperm counts.

Before the physician concludes that a semen specimen is in some way abnormal, a second semen specimen is analyzed for confirmation. If the second specimen also appears abnormal, the physician will usually advise consultation with a urologist. If, however, the husband's sperm seems adequate, the physician proceeds with further investigation of the wife.

THE SEMEN OF INFERTILE MEN

It has long been known by medical scientists that a man may be identified by his semen. Unlike the red blood cells, which are microscopically indistinguishable among the vast majority of the world's healthy individuals, spermatozoa are practically characteristic. Thus, experts claim they find it easy to recognize a man by his semen, as seen under a microscope.

The characteristic sperm pattern of a man, however, may be altered suddenly in response to: diseases, such as pneumonia and chicken pox; toxic chemical substances; medications, such as tranquilizers and antidepressants; severe allergic reactions; and heat. Not only can spermatogenesis be seriously impaired by high fever, but also by interference with normal intrascrotal cooling—taking prolonged hot baths, sitting on hot machinery, or wearing tightly woven protective clothing. Even a relatively simple and seemingly harmless fashion change in male attire could conceivably render healthy young men comparatively infertile for a time.

When spermatogenesis is adversely affected, a man's semen may contain many bizarre shapes of sperm heads, immature sperm cells, and extraneous cells that normally do not belong in semen. Genetic factors are among the causes thought to increase the percentage of abnormal forms in the semen. It has been found that the DNA content (the genetic material of the nucleus of every cell) is more or less constant from sperm to sperm in the fertile man, but deficient and variable in the sperm of infertile men and bulls.

In recent studies of men of low fertility, over two hundred different grossly abnormal forms of sperm cells have been identified. Some sperm heads were described as tapering, slipper, dumbbell, gourd-shaped, and extremely large with ragged edges. In certain semen specimens, all sperm heads were round; in others, all sperm heads were small. Sperm with kinked, bent, or coiled tails have also been seen, as well as double-headed sperm (also observed in the semen of animals such as sterile bulls), and four-headed, four-tailed sperm.

TREATMENT

Many methods of treating the infertile male have had their vogue over the past decades. Such therapies as vitamins, radiation, and testosterone have proven disappointing. Today's therapy for the most part involves improving the man's general health, controlling and eliminating infections, and advising him as to the timing and frequency of intercourse. Regular hours of sleep, exercise, and work are recommended; and for the tense, tired, overworked husband, a vacation has sometimes proved to be a specific remedy. Maintaining a nutritionally adequate diet and avoiding excesses in smoking, drinking, and intercourse are still advised.

There is specific therapy for specific conditions, such as correcting hypothyroidism with medication. Surgical treatment, particularly of varicocele, and of certain congenital or obstructive conditions often proves effective. Upon occasion, psychiatric treatment offers a cure if the inability to initiate pregnancy is due to severe premature ejaculation or erectile impotence.

Many new hormone derivatives and other types of medications are currently being tested in the treatment of male infertility. Especially encouraging has been the initial testing of menotropins (human menopausal gonadotrophin) in the relatively rare instances where there is insufficient pituitary sex-stimulating hormone.

Recently, healthy volunteers permitted daily applications of heat and/or an ice bag to the scrotum in order that experimenters could determine the effects of altered intrascrotal temperatures on spermatogenesis. Reduction in temperature was found to directly stimulate sperm output, while increased scrotal temperature produced an initial inhibition of sperm production followed by a predictable increase. Such contrived alteration of sperm production could conceivably benefit men whose sperm output is insufficient. Cold showers, while dampening ardor, may paradoxically enhance fertility.

24

Diagnosis and Treatment of Female Infertility

The complexity of a woman's physiology cannot be better illustrated than by the precisely arranged sequence of biological events essential to the fertilization of her ovum and to the subsequent birth of a baby. Successful reproduction requires an ovum to have reached maturity, to be discharged on time, to meet the sperm, to be delivered properly after fertilization to its uterine bed, to be maintained properly during embryonic and fetal life, and to be delivered safely to the outside world. Female infertility may be due to one or more adverse factors affecting any part of this long and intricate chain of processes. Although the causes of female infertility outnumber by far the causes of male infertility, modern medicine much of the time offers more diverse and effective treatment for the infertile woman than for her male counterpart.

NORMAL OVARIAN FUNCTION

Nature provides the human female infant *at birth* with her lifetime supply of oocytes, immature egg cells that subsequently develop into mature ova. The mystery of oogenesis is exemplified by the fact that of the hundreds of thousands of oocytes present when a girl child is born, proportionately few develop to maturity and still fewer are ejected from the ovary as eggs capable of being fertilized by sperm. It is estimated that, in the approximately thirty years of a woman's reproductive life, no more than 390 of these ova are "ovulated." How and why these few are selected from the many, and whether this selection process serves a specific purpose or is a statistical accident of nature, remain unknown.

At the time of puberty the pituitary gonadotrophic* hormones—FSH (follicle-stimulating hormone) and LH (luteinizing hormone)—trigger the mechanism for the onset of menstruation. In the United States, the menarche (first period) usually arrives when a girl is between the ages of eleven and fourteen, although occasionally a normally developed girl will not have her first period until the age of sixteen. The first few menstrual periods are usually not accompanied by ovulation and tend to be irregular. A regular menstrual pattern is not established until ovulation becomes cyclic.

The two ovaries, whose chief physiologic role is reproduction, are located in the lower part of the abdomen in the pelvis, one on each side of the uterus. They are shaped like almonds and measure on the average of 1½ inches in length, 1 inch in breadth, and ½ inch in thickness. The process of ovulation begins when FSH and LH stimulate an egg cell, surrounded by a small sac known as a follicle, to go to the surface of the ovary where the follicle opens and releases the ripened egg. The ovarian tissues surrounding the egg, in turn,

---

* In Greek, *gonos* means "a sex gland" and *trephein* means "to nourish."

manufacture two hormones of their own—estrogen and progesterone. It is the successive effects of these two hormones on the endometrium (the lining of the uterus) that cause menstruation if the egg is not fertilized.

The endometrium, a pinkish, velvety membrane, can vary in thickness from two hundredths of an inch to two tenths of an inch, depending upon the amount of estrogen and progesterone acting on it. The blood supply of the endometrium comes from the myometrium (the muscle of the uterus) and consists of straight and coiled arteries, the straight supplying the base of the uterine lining and the coiled supplying the surface layers. Estrogen, which causes the lining to swell and the coiled arteries to open up, is followed by progesterone, which heightens the effect of the estrogen by making the lining more swollen and "riper." The endometrium is then ready to receive a fertilized egg and to nourish it as it develops into an embryo, fetus, and baby.

The majority of the egg cells that leave the ovaries are not fertilized; after reaching the uterus, they disintegrate and disappear. The successive rise in ovarian hormones not only affects the uterine lining, but acts to turn off the pituitary gonadotrophic hormones. There follows a sharp diminution in ovarian hormones, causing the blood supply of the thickened top layers of the endometrium to be cut off. Thus, endometrial tissue and blood are shed through the vagina as menstrual flow. The straight arteries that supply the base of the endometrium remain unaffected during the entire process, maintaining the health of the bottom of the uterine lining so the next menstrual cycle is able to begin. The pituitary hormones and the ovarian hormones maintain this circular feedback system throughout a woman's reproductive life, "changing" due to gradual decline of ovarian hormonal function until menstruation no longer occurs. In the United States ovulation in most women begins to falter around the age of forty-five. Menopause, the end of menstruation, takes place at the average age of forty-nine, but may occur in a healthy woman before age thirty-six and after age fifty-five.

INVESTIGATION OF THE OVARIAN FACTOR

Due to the dual basic functions of the ovary—the cyclic release of ova and the production of ovarian hormones—diagnostic tests are performed on the wife to determine if she ovulates and with what regularity, and if her endocrine system (for the manufacture of essential hormones) is functioning normally. For this purpose, the following tests may be performed:

BASAL BODY TEMPERATURE (BBT)

A daily record is kept for two or more cycles of the "basal" body temperature, taken in the usual way but upon awakening and before any activity. If ovulation has taken place, a sharp rise in temperature will have been noted, usually between Day 12 and Day 16 of the cycle, thought to be due to the action of progesterone. The temperature rise, however, is only an approximate guide to the time of ovulation, which may actually have occurred 48–72 hours before.

ENDOMETRIAL BIOPSY

Tissue from the endometrium is obtained under anaesthesia in a procedure similar to a "D and C." It is usually performed premenstrually, or any time after Day 26 in a 28–30-day cycle. If ovulation has taken place, the biopsy will show endometrial tissue that has been properly "primed" by appropriate estrogen and progesterone stimulation. If ovulation has not occurred, the specimen fails to show any of the changes that are conducive to proper nourishment of the fertilized egg. If ovulation has been indicated by the basal body temperature over a period of three to four months and by endometrial biopsy, the woman is usually instructed to discontinue the recording of her temperature.

FERN TEST

Two specimens of cervical mucus are examined, one in the middle of the menstrual cycle and the other shortly before the onset of menstruation, for evidence of ovulation. This test is based on the fact that mucus secreted by glands of the endocervix (inner part of the cervix), when allowed to dry on a glass slide, exhibits a distinctive fern-like pattern at the time of peak estrogen levels. However, the presence of progesterone abolishes it. If the first specimen shows typical fern formation and the second shows no ferning, it is assumed ovulation has taken place. If the second specimen shows continued ferning, it is presumed that ovulation did not occur.

VAGINAL SMEAR SERIES

Vaginal smears are taken daily (usually by the woman herself) from Day 5 to Day 20 of the cycle and examined for evidence of the changing balance of estrogen and progesterone associated with ovulation. If ovulation has occurred, such cell changes may also indicate the approximate time it took place.

URINARY PREGNANEDIOL TEST

Between Day 22 and Day 24, urine is collected over a 24-hour period and the level of pregnanediol is measured. The amount of this derivative of progesterone excreted in the urine during this time indicates whether ovulation has taken place.

If one or more of the tests for ovulation discloses that a woman does ovulate, the basal body temperature may be used to determine the time of ovulation. The couple is then often instructed to have intercourse at that time to enhance their chances of initiating a pregnancy.

Attempts to improve on the reliability and accuracy of basal body temperature measurements taken orally, rectally, or vaginally have led at least one group of researchers to develop an electronic system for continuously measuring and recording the basal temperature. A tiny, watertight, battery-operated radio transmitter—sensitive to temperature—is mounted on the rim of an arcing-spring diaphragm whose dome has been removed to allow for intercourse, conception, or menstruation. This domeless diaphragm is inserted into the vaginal vault, where it can be worn continuously for periods of up to a year. There is also a similar type of transmitter packaged like a tampon for vaginal insertion. While the transmitter tampon does not require fitting like the transmitter diaphragm, it must be removed for intercourse and menstruation. With either type of transmitter, the antenna receiving the transmitted temperature recordings—a flat spiral coil the approximate size of the woman's bed—is placed on a firm board and inserted beneath the mattress. The output of the antenna is then fed to a recorder at the bedside, which indicates the variations in temperature on a slow-running strip chart and can even be connected to an alarm device to audibly signal the anticipated temperature rise.

TREATMENT OF OVARIAN DISORDERS

If the tests disclose that a woman's cycles are anovulatory (without ovulation), the physician will investigate possible causes for failure of ovulation. Abnormalities of pituitary, adrenal, or thyroid function may be responsible, and in many cases, can be treated. If the pituitary, adrenal, and thyroid functions are found to be normal, and if no specific cause could be diagnosed to explain anovulation, the physician may then try to induce ovulation by one of several new pharmacologic methods.

In an effort to temporarily suppress the pituitary-ovarian hormonal circular feedback, oral synthetic progestogen-estrogen therapy (The Pill) is given for three to four menstrual cycles, one tablet daily from Day 5 through Day 24. After medication is discontinued, ovulation may be initiated in about ten percent of cases.

Several years ago a non-steroid compound, *clomiphene citrate*, was found to inhibit ovulation in rats, and clinical trials were begun to test it as an oral contraceptive. Within a short time, it became apparent that this potent drug, instead of being an antifertility agent, surprisingly enhanced fertility potential by inducing ovulation in women who were not having their menstrual periods. Clomiphene citrate has an unusual ability, for reasons unknown, to stimulate secretion of pituitary gonadotrophins, and in anovulatory women who have normal estrogen levels (as determined by the fern test or vaginal smears), it has been shown to induce ovulation in approximately seventy percent.

Potentially even better than clomiphene citrate for inducing ovulation may be a newly developed approach in gonadotrophic therapy. Although gonadotrophins from animal pituitaries have been employed in treating gynecological and other types of disorders for over three decades, human gonadotrophins from the urine of menopausal women (HMG) in conjunction with human gonadotrophins from the urine of pregnant women (HCG) are succeeding in many instances of previously untreatable infertility. Women who were treated with animal products developed antibodies which inactivated the animal gonadotrophins. Such a reaction has not occurred with the use of human gonadotrophins. This new treatment for female infertility is referred to as HMG-HCG therapy. At present, it is not available to the public, but is under investigation by the Food and Drug Administration.

One researcher has attempted transplantation of healthy ovarian tissues from women undergoing voluntary sterilization to women with abnormal or nonfunctioning ovaries. If successful, this surgical technique could open up a vast new area for restoration of ovarian function, induction of ovulation, treatment of menopause, and prevention of the transmission of maternal genetic defects by the substitution of other, genetically different oocytes or egg cells.

INVESTIGATION OF THE CERVICAL FACTOR

Infertility may be caused by interference with proper placement of semen into the cervix. Since such factors as hormonal imbalance, anatomic defects, or infectious conditions can present a barrier against conception, diagnostic tests are performed on the wife to determine if any such cervical abnormality is present. The penetration of sperm through the female cervical mucus is an extremely complex phenomenon that involves the physical structure of the mucus, the motility of the sperm, and mutual interactions between mucus and sperm.

POSTCOITAL TEST (SIMS-HUHNER TEST)

After intercourse during the fertile phase of the wife's menstrual cycle, the wife is seen within six hours by her physician and a specimen of her cervical mucus is obtained from far up in the endocervical canal, where sperm motility and survival are at a maximum. Normally, the cervical mucus at mid-cycle increases in *spinnbarkeit* (stretchability), favoring sperm penetration. To demonstrate spinnbarkeit, the cervical mucus is stretched or pulled apart to form as long a continuous thread as possible. The Sims-Huhner test, a microscopic examination of the cervical mucus, assays various factors necessary for insemination. Adequate concentration of living sperm in the specimen establishes that there is no anatomic or mechanical interference with the depositing of sperm. The postcoital specimen can also indicate the presence of such conditions as infection, or trauma of the cervix, inadequate estrogen stimulation of cervical tissue, deficient spermatozoa, and antibody reaction between cervical secretions and sperm.

SEMEN PENETRATION TEST (MILLER-KURZROCK TEST)

This simple procedure helps to recognize any existing "hostility" in the cervical mucus to spermatozoa. A drop of the husband's semen is placed on a slide just next to a drop of the wife's cervical mucus obtained at the calculated time of ovulation. Under the microscope the penetration of the mucus by the sperm can be observed, as well as the duration of sperm viability. If the sperm dies or does not penetrate the mucus, cervical hostility is presumed. An abnormal postcoital or semen penetration test, despite good evidence of ovulation obtained from a fern test, suggests the presence of immunological factors such as ABO incompatibility.

TREATMENT OF CERVICAL DISORDERS

Cervical hostility due to estrogen deficiency may be treated by a course of small oral doses of estrogen to improve the cervical mucus without inhibiting ovulation. If the cause of cervical hostility is due to an immunological reaction between the cervical secretions and the husband's sperm, the couple is advised to abstain from intercourse or to use condoms for a six-month period, with the expectation that the wife's antibody reactions will be diminished during this time.

Certain anatomic abnormalities that interfere with depositing or penetration of sperm may be repaired surgically. For example, cervical stenosis, or a closed cervix, may be relieved by surgical dilatation, which then allows sperm to enter the cervical canal. Endocervicitis, inflammation and infection of the cervical canal, is also treated by dilatation and a course of antibiotics, often along with antifungal agents. Cervical polyps, or growths obstructing the vagina and cervix, are treated by cauterization or surgical removal—almost always an office procedure. Vaginismus, spasm of the vaginal muscles, may be due to emotional factors and, in most cases, usually responds best to psychotherapy. Sometimes hard bands of vaginal tissue prevent successful intercourse and must be corrected surgically.

The incompetent internal os (opening) of the cervix, usually referred to as "incompetent cervix," is a major cause of secondary infertility. In this condition the opening between the uterine cavity and the cervical canal is abnormally large, preventing a pregnancy from proceeding to term. A woman with an incompetent cervix has a history of one or more pregnancies in which spontaneous abortion (miscarriage) has occurred beyond the first trimester. An incompetent cervix can be caused by a number of factors, including an abnormally short cervix, injury to the cervix from a difficult labor, certain fibroid tumors, and hormonal imbalance. Since the first successful surgical repair of an incompetent cervix was performed in 1941, operations now done—in certain cases when the woman is not pregnant and in others during pregnancy—offer a better than eighty-five percent chance that a pregnancy will continue to term.

INVESTIGATION OF THE TUBAL FACTOR

To ensure the proper meeting of ovum and sperm, the fallopian tubes must be normal in structure and function. The ovum, usually fertilized in the outer third of the tube, is nourished by tubal secretions and transported by the tube to the uterus on a fairly rigid schedule—within five or six days of ovulation—if it is to be successfully implanted. To determine whether the wife's tubes are patent (free from obstruction), one or more of the following examinations may be made:

TUBAL INSUFFLATION (THE RUBIN TEST)

This method of testing tubal patency has been performed for over twenty-five years and is usually done in the doctor's office. During the week following menstruation, the cervix, uterus, and tubes are inflated with carbon dioxide under measured pressure. Tubal patency of at least one tube is indicated when the graph on the inflator registers a gradual rise then fall in pressure; it is confirmed when the woman experiences shoulder discomfort from the carbon dioxide which has been blown through the tube or tubes into the abdomen, giving referred pain in the shoulder. If the graph registers a sharp increasing rise in pressure with *no* decline, tubal obstruction is present.

HYSTEROSALPINGOGRAPHY

Radiopaque material is introduced through the cervix to outline the uterus and tubes so these organs can be examined by fluoroscopy or X-ray films. Hysterosalpingograms may demonstrate tubal patency or verify a diagnosis of tubal obstruction. In the latter case, the location and often the cause of the obstruction can be determined.

CULDOSCOPY

This hospital procedure is considered by most authorities to be the most reliable diagnostic method in determining the condition of the tubes. An instrument called a culdoscope is inserted high into the vaginal canal, allowing the physician to have a direct view of the reproductive organs. While the culdoscope is in place, a colored dye is injected under pressure through the cervical canal, making it possible for the tubes to be visualized. Tubal patency can be confirmed by observing flow of the dye out through the open ovarian end of the tube. If the tube is obstructed, the exact place of obstruction may be seen. With the panculdoscope, a newer version of the culdoscope, the physician can photograph the internal reproductive organs as well.

TREATMENT OF TUBAL DISORDERS

Two of the tests previously described for determining tubal function—tubal insufflation and hysterosalpingography—are often used for the treatment of tubal obstruction. These tests are frequently used together in a combined method of treatment, hysterosalpingography being performed first, followed by carbon dioxide insufflation. Antispasmodic medication is sometimes given in conjunction with tubal insufflation to relax the muscle walls of the tubes.

Another method of treating tubal obstruction is hydrotubation—introduction of salt solution (with or without an antibiotic or cortisone preparation) through the cervix into the uterus and tubes. Hydrotubation and the combined method of hysterosalpingography-tubal insufflation have each been estimated to restore tubal patency in fifteen percent of women treated.

When these medical measures fail to restore tubal patency, reconstructive tubal surgery is often performed. New surgical techniques, including the use of polyethylene and inert plastic (Teflon) for artificial replacement of tubal parts, are producing far better results than in the past. In recent reports, success rates of tubal surgery have been estimated to be as high as thirty percent.

INVESTIGATION OF THE UTERINE FACTOR

The structure and function of the uterus and its endometrial lining must be normal for sperm to pass into the fallopian tubes and for the fertilized egg to take root and grow. A thorough pelvic examination, a record of the wife's basal body temperature, endometrial biopsy, and hysterosalpingography (all previously described) are the procedures that give important information as to uterine "normalcy."

Pelvic examination and hysterosalpingography may disclose such uterine abnormalities as fibroid tumors, endometrial polyps, and congenital malformations. More than thirty-five years ago congenital uterine malformations were reported to occur in 1 in 7,000 women. Since the use of X-ray studies of the uterus (hysterography), such malformations as double uterus have been found to occur in about 1 in 100 women. This term indicates the existence of two divided endometrial cavities, either in a single uterus or in two divided uterine bodies.

Endometrial biopsy reflects the hormonal balance of the endometrium, and the presence of scarring or infection. The basal body temperature, determining whether or when ovulation has occurred, enables the physician to determine the ideal date for biopsy. Endometrial tissue is then compared to what is normal for this time in the cycle.

TREATMENT OF UTERINE DISORDERS

Women with a history of habitual abortion (three or more consecutive spontaneous abortions) whose progesterone activity is shown to be inadequate may be helped by oral synthetic progestogens. Some physicians feel that progesterone replacement therapy should continue in pregnancy at least until the time when the placenta can be assumed to be producing this hormone, usually in the second trimester.

Tumors of the uterine muscle (myomata) and large fibroid tumors that interfere with pregnancy are removed surgically. Myomectomy is reported to have success rates as high as fifty percent in improving fertility. Displacements, or improper positions of the uterus, are sometimes corrected by means of a pessary inserted vaginally to support the uterus.

Double uterus is a frequent cause of habitual abortion, prematurity, and complications of labor. The first successful surgical unification of a double uterus was done over sixty years ago. Since that time the operation (metroplasty) has been increasingly performed, and according to recent figures, approximately eighty-five percent of women after metroplasty have completed pregnancies terminating in living children. The woman born with a double uterus, once it has been unified, seems as capable of producing living babies almost as often as the woman born with a normal uterus.

ARTIFICIAL INSEMINATION

Man, having for centuries used artificial insemination in the breeding of animals, has turned its abilities to further practical advantages by improving the quality of stock. References to unintentional human artificial insemination date back to the Talmud, the authoritative body of Jewish law and tradition. It was not until 1785, however, that the English physiologist and surgeon John Hunter initiated the practice of inseminating a woman with her husband's semen. In the United States, husband insemination was carried out by Dr. Marion Sims in 1866; and in 1890, Dr. Robert L. Dickinson, a pioneer in sex education, birth control, and marriage counseling, performed the first insemination using the semen of a donor instead of the husband.

Artificial insemination is performed today for infertile couples when other methods of initiating a pregnancy have failed. Husband insemination is usually performed in cases where the husband's semen is normal, but the wife's cervix is abnormal either in structure or function. Donor insemination is recommended: 1) when the husband's semen is found upon examination to be inadequate for conception; 2) in certain instances when Rh incompatibility has already resulted in an infant with erythroblastosis; 3) when the husband's family history of genetic disease poses a serious threat to the potential normalcy of his own children; 4) when the couple's previous children demonstrated genetic disease; and 5) when both husband and wife have been shown to have reduced fertility and all other medical help has not been successful.

Donors are chosen from groups of highly fertile men of various ethnic and religious backgrounds who are genetically well endowed, physically and intellectually. The identity of the donor and the couple is kept completely anonymous from one another. Therapeutic donor insemination has been increasing in use for the past twenty years, as well as growing in social acceptance. The state of Oklahoma is till now the only state to have passed laws regarding donor insemination, legitimizing its practice and establishing the legitimacy of children born after such fertility treatment. Other states are expected to follow.

Semen, frozen and stored, has already been the source of a number of children. The first research on frozen human semen is said to date back to 1776 when the Italian experimental biologist Lazzaro Spallanzani observed that spermatozoa cooled by snow became motionless during cooling but revived on warming. In 1866 Italian physiologist and anthropologist Paolo Mantegazza was successful in freezing human semen at $-15°$ C. He originated the concept of banks for frozen human semen, suggesting that a dying man on a battlefield might sire a legal heir with his semen frozen and stored at home. Since the 1940's, researchers have experimented with many techniques for the preservation and freezing of human and animal sperm. Scientists are now able to freeze and store human semen at $-196°$ C. and still achieve an average of seventy percent recovery of motile sperm after more than four years—and with no apparent damage to genetic mechanisms.

Frozen-storage of human sperm could enable husbands with inadequate sperm counts to have their ejaculates collected and stored for a period of several months, then thawed, pooled, and concentrated for insemination at sperm concentrations many times greater than any of their single ejaculates.

The chances of a woman's ovum being successfully fertilized by either husband or donor semen could be improved by using stored semen for four or more consecutive days at the time when ovulation is most likely to occur.

Perhaps the most dramatic use of stored semen could be the realization of Mantegazza's prediction of a man being able to induce conception ages after death.

PART VII

THE OLDER WOMAN

25

The Menopause

Preoccupation with the menopause is a recent development in the history of womankind. After approximately 800,000 years of human evolution, women had a life expectancy of twenty-five years in Roman times. More than a thousand years passed before it increased to just over thirty years of age. By the turn of the twentieth century, life expectancy had risen to a little less than fifty years. A girl baby born in 1969 can expect to live to be almost eighty, approximately ten years longer than a boy baby born today—following the pattern in which the female in many known species outlives the male. Improvements in nutrition, sanitation, and medical science have bestowed upon the modern woman the unique distinction of belonging to the only species of mammals in which most females far outlive their reproductive capacity. Many women, in fact, spend more years of their lives without ovarian function than with it.

Complex hormonal shifts change a girl into a woman at puberty, a woman into a mother during pregnancy, and terminate a woman's reproductive life at the menopause. The end of ovarian function and its accompanying drop in a woman's supply of estrogens is not the *cause* of a woman's aging, as is commonly believed. Aging is a combination of genetic, environmental, and constitutional factors. The aging process starts shortly after birth. The human female continues to age—in spite of normal estrogen activity from puberty until the approach of menopause.

WHAT "CHANGE OF LIFE" MEANS

"Change of life," or the *climacteric* (from the Greek meaning "rung of a ladder," "a critical time"), refers to the span of time during which decline in ovarian function takes place—usually ranging from age forty to sixty. The *menopause* literally means cessation of menses, or menstrual periods. Each woman is unique, and how a woman is affected physically and emotionally during this period depends upon her biological and psychological makeup. Much of how a woman goes through her "change of life" is a reflection of her attitudes about herself, her family life, her fulfillment as a woman, and her success in achieving certain personal goals. While the climacteric can cause many minor disturbances and a few severe disorders requiring medical attention, most women stop menstruating with little or no ill effects.

Menstruation occasionally comes to an end abruptly; more commonly, there is a gradual cessation. The usual pattern—to skip one or two periods, to have normal periods for a few months, and then to skip periods once more—may be repeated many times until the menopause actually occurs. During this process, the amount and duration of menstrual flow may be the same as normal, or there may be a lessening in both.

MENOPAUSAL SYMPTOMS AND TREATMENT

Symptoms attributed to change of life fall into three categories: 1) changes in the autonomic nervous system (hot flushes, sweats, palpitations, gastrointestinal complaints, numbness and tingling in the extremities); 2) physical changes (menstrual disorders, loss of skin elasticity, weight gain, vaginitis, reduced size of breasts and external genitalia, muscular and skeletal pains); and 3) psychosomatic complaints (headaches, insomnia, nervousness, dizziness, fatigue, anxiety, depression, crying spells, lessening of the sex drive).

For more than three decades physicians have used estrogens to treat all menopausal symptoms. Until recently, the treatment was conservative—small amounts of estrogens for brief periods of time. The current attitude of many doctors is to prescribe prolonged estrogen replacement, depending upon the particular needs of the individual woman. After one or more three-week courses of estrogens, some women are no longer bothered with hot flushes or other discomforts. Other women require much longer estrogen therapy to feel their best. In certain cases, progesterone is given in conjunction with estrogen therapy.

To help determine the amount of estrogen a woman may need, the physician may make several studies of cells taken from the upper vagina in the same way a vaginal smear is taken for the Papanicolaou cancer detection test. These vaginal smears, along with specific physical findings, provide the doctor with a basis for estimating the degree of a woman's estrogenic activity.

The fear that estrogens can produce cancer is based in part on a thirty-year-old experiment on cancer-susceptible mice, and has been a subject of medical debate since that time. There has been to date, however, no strong evidence to indicate that estrogen can initiate cancer in humans. Some physicians have speculated that estrogens may stimulate the development of a cancer present *before* estrogen replacement therapy was begun. Yet, there has been a recent suggestion that a certain type of estrogen therapy may even prevent breast cancer. Coronary heart disease, also, is thought by many to be preventable by maintaining adequate amounts of estrogens. (A regimen of estrogens in men has appeared to prevent the progression of coronary heart disease, but the doses required often produce feminization and loss of their sexual potency.) Osteoporosis, thinning of the bones and loss of calcium, occurs most frequently in postmenopausal women and can, in varying degrees, be prevented by estrogen therapy. Sometimes estrogens are given for whatever possible cosmetic effects may be achieved.

Mild psychosomatic menopausal symptoms frequently respond well not only to estrogens but also to sedatives, tranquilizers, or antidepressant medication. Sometimes a brief period of psychotherapy can be very beneficial.

CHANGE AND "CHANGE OF LIFE"

In the days when woman's reproductive function was her dominant life force, a strongly negative reaction to the menopause was to be expected. Today this feeling is changing. A woman's increased life span, the relative decrease in importance of her solely reproductive capacity in an overpopulated world, the variety of personally rewarding occupations now available to the mature woman, and the greater possibilities for enjoyment of leisure time have brought about this change. By helping the older woman avoid many uncomfortable and some incapacitating complications of the climacteric, modern medicine is enabling her to anticipate the years ahead with better health and more joy in living.

26

Diagnosis and Treatment of Breast Cancer

Since 1930 there has been a slow but steady rise in the national death rate from cancer. While the incidence of leukemia, cancer of the pancreas, and lung cancer (the leading cause of cancer deaths in the United States since 1954) has increased, the incidence of breast cancer has remained essentially unchanged during this period. The increasing use of estrogens for the menopause and of the hormones contained in oral contraceptives apparently has not affected breast cancer statistics.

The most common cancer in the human female, breast cancer, has been estimated by the American Cancer Society to afflict six percent of all American women. It rarely occurs in young women; the majority of cases are in women over forty. The risk of developing cancer of the breast is felt to be slightly higher in women with a family history of the disease, or in women who have never been pregnant or did not breastfeed their children, or whose menopause was abnormally late.

Early diagnosis greatly improves the chances of a cure in many cases, and toward that goal a number of new diagnostic procedures are currently being utilized.

MAMMOGRAPHY

Mammography is a special type of X-ray examination of the breast that has been used in an increasing number of medical centers since the early 1960's for the diagnosis of breast diseases. Because a mammogram is able to reveal the presence of a cancer that has produced neither signs nor symptoms, it could become a routine diagnostic test for the screening of breast cancer. While a skilled physician is unlikely to feel a growth as small as 1 cm. in diameter, mammography is able to discover a lesion as small as 0.5 cm., and has been shown to be an especially sensitive technique for detecting tiny cancerous growths in older women with large breasts.

Mammography is also helpful in excluding the possibility of cancer in certain cases where a lump or mass may have been felt by a doctor or by the woman herself.

THERMOGRAPHY

Used principally since 1961 for the diagnosis of breast cancer, thermography is a photographic technique employing infrared cameras (sensitive to heat) for the recording of localized skin temperature. As fever recorded by a thermometer usually signifies illness, warm areas or "hot spots" on the skin recorded by thermography can signify the presence of disease. Similarly, as a thermometer cannot specify the cause of a fever, a thermogram's recording of a hot spot cannot specify a particular disease, for several ailments affecting breast tissue other than cancer can also be responsible for skin temperature elevations. Thermography has been used in large cancer-screening programs, and in more than ninety percent of cases in which cancer was found, this new diagnostic technique had revealed the presence of a localized hot spot over the lesion.

Like mammography, thermography is also helpful in excluding the possibility of cancer or other breast diseases. In the past year or two, thermography has been used along with mammography in a combined method for even better sensitivity in the detection of early breast cancer.

XEROGRAPHY

Xerography is another technique of securing an X-ray image of the breast for cancer detection. Instead of using standard X-ray photographic film (as in mammography), xerographic X-rays are made on specially treated 10" x 17" metal plates similar to the type used in office copying machines. After X-ray exposure, the plate is developed under a cloud of oppositely-charged powder in a lightproof box.

A xerogram shows all the tissues of the breast, including the skin, in a single exposure. Many details that are difficult to see on a mammogram are revealed on a xerogram. However, the equipment for performing xerography has at this time not been adapted for general use.

ULTRASONIC HOLOGRAPHIC BEAMS

The latest approach to early detection of breast cancer is the projected use of ultrasonic holographic beams. Two ultrasonic beams of the same frequency are passed through breast tissue to obtain a ripple pattern produced by the interference of the beams. This, in turn, yields a three-dimensional image of internal tissue that can be viewed directly. Having been successful in detecting implanted tumors in rats and mice, this new technique is soon to be tested on human subjects.

TREATMENT OF BREAST CANCER

The treatment of breast cancer may consist of one or a combination of therapies. The most common treatment of breast cancer in women of all ages is *radical mastectomy*, complete removal of the affected breast and adjacent lymph nodes—following proof that there is no spread of the disease (metastasis) to other areas. In patients with local spread (local metastases), a combination of radical mastectomy plus radiotherapy (X-ray or cobalt) may be used. Simple mastectomy, complete removal of the affected breast without removal of adjacent tissues, and simple mastectomy plus radiotherapy are performed less frequently. Radiotherapy alone is used to treat inoperable lesions, and has proven effective in many cases.

Premenopausal women are sometimes treated additionally by oophorectomy, removal of the ovaries, or hypophysectomy, removal of the pituitary gland. These procedures are rarely performed on older women because of their changed hormonal status.

In postmenopausal women with advanced breast cancer, hormonal therapy—usually estrogens—is often effective. Male hormones, androgens, also have a distinctive place in the management of women with advanced disease.

In addition to hormones, there is a steadily growing number of drugs—chemotherapy—which have been shown to control the disease for varying periods of time.

In previous days it was not uncommon for women who underwent breast cancer surgery to be left with a clumsy and unsightly swollen arm on the side of the operation. This has become a much rarer consequence following today's improved surgical techniques. It is now routine for a woman who has undergone mastectomy to be fitted with a breast form to restore her normal appearance.

DETECTION OF UTERINE CANCER

Uterine cancer, including cancer of the cervix (the neck of the uterus), is usually fatal if allowed to reach advanced stages. However, its detection in the early stages and prompt treatment can bring an almost 100 percent cure.

The late Dr. George N. Papanicolaou's test for cervical cancer, usually referred to as the Pap smear, is a simple cellular examination that detects the presence of uterine cancer long before symptoms appear. Wider use of the Papanicolaou test and improved methods of treating early uterine cancer have resulted over the last two decades in a continuously declining death rate from uterine cancer in the United States.

27

Cosmetic Surgery

The human desire to look more attractive is as old as mankind itself, and the use of surgery for this purpose is recorded in the history of ancient India and Egypt. Throughout the centuries surgical techniques were devised to improve man's appearance, but it was not until the Renaissance that plastic surgery came into its own as a medical specialty—mainly through the efforts of Gasparo di Tagliacozzi, who is called the father of modern plastic surgery. Not only did he introduce dramatic new technical improvements, but he recognized the profound emotional impact of his kind of surgery upon the patient. In *The Surgery of Defects by Implantation*, first published in 1597, he wrote: "We restore, repair, and make whole those parts of the face which nature has given but which Fortune has taken away, not so much that they may delight the eye but that they may buoy up the spirit and help the mind of the afflicted."

Each society has its particular standards of physical attractiveness, and a striking deviation from these standards often prevents an individual from being wholly accepted in his society. For example, on several remote South Pacific islands adult natives of Melanesian extraction do not consider such defects as cleft palate and cleft lip socially unacceptable. However, it is considered a misfortune if a member of their group is born with straight and not crinkly hair; and, therefore, much emphasis is placed on proper crinkling of the hair. In addition, hair dyes have been widely used to keep gray hair hidden.

The concept of one's appearance in relation to behavior and personality has become a significant consideration in modern psychology. The body image, a frame of reference for a person's reaction to his environment, greatly influences his emotional life. Increasing numbers of people of all ages and both sexes, dissatisfied with certain facial or body features, are taking advantage of the greater variety and better techniques offered by modern cosmetic surgery.

NOSE SURGERY

Plastic surgery of the nose, or rhinoplasty, is the most commonly performed cosmetic operation. In most cases the nose is shortened, any hump reduced by removal of excess cartilage and bone, and the nostrils often reshaped. This kind of procedure is also done to correct breathing difficulties due to a deviated septum or other structural nasal abnormalities.

Surgical correction of a receding chin, or menoplasty, is frequently performed in conjunction with nasal reconstruction to improve the facial balance. Cartilage or bone transplants, or silicone-rubber implants, may be used to extend the contour of the chin. These same reconstructive materials are also utilized to rebuild noses flattened as a result of injury.

A rhinoplasty usually takes about an hour to perform and requires about three days in the hospital. It is not generally done before the age of sixteen or after the age of sixty, although it can be done later in life, depending upon the person's general health.

EYELID SURGERY

Plastic surgery of the eyelids, or blepharoplasty, is performed to correct malformations of the eyelids present from birth or caused by injury. Such a procedure can be done on a very small child with drooping upper lids that cannot fully open. In a similar manner, the normally formed Mongoloid eyelids of Orientals can be changed to resemble those of Caucasians—an operation that has been frequently performed in Japan since World War II.

Disfiguring bags under the eyes—a characteristic that sometimes runs in families but occasionally is related to disturbed thyroid-pituitary relationship—can be surgically corrected (as can sagging lower lids). These "bags" are hernias of fatty tissue through the eye-closing muscles. Blepharoplasty of all four eyelids, whether performed on men or women, usually takes between one and two hours and requires about three days in the hospital.

FACE-LIFT

Plastic surgery to remove wrinkles and skin folds, or rhytidectomy (*rhytid* is Greek for "wrinkle"), is most frequently performed in women between the ages of fifty and seventy. An incision is made near the ears and behind the hairline; skin from the face and neck is lifted up and tightened, and excess skin is trimmed away. As loss of skin elasticity usually accompanies the aging process, a person may eventually desire another face-lift, which can be done five to ten years after the first operation. Rhytidectomy usually takes from four to five hours to perform and requires about a week in the hospital.

Deep furrows, or frown wrinkles, between the eyebrows

may be removed by the insertion of a specially prepared skin graft.

ABRASIVE FACIAL SKIN TREATMENTS

Chemabrasion, or chemosurgery—the use of chemicals to peel off the top layer of skin—is a method of facial rejuvenation that does not completely remove wrinkles, but can improve the general appearance of the forehead, eyelids, and upper face. It is sometimes used alone or in conjunction with surgical face-lift procedures for the lower face and neck.

Dermabrasion is another technique for removing the top layer of skin. It employs abrasives which, like sandpaper on wood, can smooth a roughened surface. Dermabrasion is mainly used in the treatment of skin scarred by acne and to remove pursing wrinkles about the mouth.

EAR SURGERY

Plastic surgery of the ear, or otoplasty, is performed on children and adults with oversized or protruding ears, or to replace an ear missing from birth or due to injury. It is preferable for children to have the operation before they start school to avoid their being teased by other children. Otoplasty usually takes about an hour and rarely requires more than one day of hospitalization.

BREAST SURGERY

Although the female breast and its form had social and cultural (as well as biological) significance in many ancient cultures, there is no record that in these early times any surgical attempts were made to alter breast shape to any accepted standard. It was not until the middle of the nineteenth century that a Parisian surgeon described procedures to change breast size and shape. Since that time, surgeons in Europe and the United States have devised cosmetic breast operations that can be performed on women between the ages of twenty and seventy.

In *reduction mammaplasty* oversized breasts, which can be painful or cause poor posture, are made smaller by removal of excess skin and breast tissue, often necessitating reimplantation of the nipple. As much as seven pounds of tissue may be removed from each breast. This operation for reducing breast size and weight is an intricate surgical procedure, usually lasting three to four hours and requiring an average of eight to ten days in the hospital. Sensation recovers in the transplanted nipple.

In *augmentation mammaplasty* underdeveloped breasts are made larger by implants of plastic material. An incision is made at the underfold of the breast, creating a pocket between the breast tissue and the muscles of the chest wall. Into this pocket is inserted a silicone-rubber bag containing a silicone gel, or in some cases, a silicone-rubber bag filled from the outside with an antiseptic solution. An operation for augmenting breast size is a relatively simple procedure, usually taking between one and two hours to perform and requiring about a week's stay in the hospital.

Injection into the breast of paraffin—a treatment for breast-enlarging that originated in Germany in the 1880's and became popular in Japan after World War II—is not considered an acceptable procedure in the United States because of subsequent formation of tumors from the paraffin. Also controversial in this country because of possible tumor formation is the injection into the breast of liquid silicone, which has a tendency to move around and to cause the breasts to sag.

LESS COMMON PROCEDURES

A too-prominent lower jaw, or prognathism, may be surgically corrected by the removal of sections of the jawbone. This is generally done in conjunction with orthodontic treatment in which the teeth are realigned.

An extremely complicated procedure is the removal of deforming fat deposits from the buttocks, abdomen, and upper arms. Similar to a face-lift in which the skin is lifted and tightened, removal of body fat may take between two and five hours and may require as long as two weeks of hospitalization.

SEX-EXCHANGE SURGERY

Rare in number but most unhappy are those individuals who from an early age have suffered from a conflict over their sexual identification. It is difficult for a person who has never questioned his maleness or her femaleness to understand the plight of someone who feels there has been an error in his or her gender identity. Although there have always been some few people, male and female, who have sought to "change their sex," it was not until the early 1950's that *transsexualism* came to public attention as a result of the sensational publicity given to Christine Jorgensen's "sex change" operation in Copenhagen.

Confusion in gender identity is particularly characteristic of the homosexual, the transvestite (one who derives sexual enjoyment from wearing clothes of the opposite sex), and the transsexual. All have doubts about their assigned sexual roles, but each differs from the other in a number of ways. Unlike the homosexual and transvestite, who take pleasure in their sex organs, the male or female transsexual considers his or her sex organs as disturbing deformities and will go so far as to threaten or attempt suicide to obtain surgical correction.

Although "sex transformation" surgery has been performed in foreign countries for some time, only recently has it begun to be performed in the United States, at The Johns Hopkins Hospital in Baltimore and several other medical centers across the country. Johns Hopkins has also established a so-called Gender Identity Clinic, in which the role of surgery for transsexuals is evaluated by a special committee of psychiatrists, psychologists, plastic surgeons, urologists, and gynecologists. This group carefully screen applicants and select a few individuals over the age of twenty-one for the sex-exchange surgery in the expectation of offering them more contented lives. Both male and female transsexuals who undergo sex-reassignment surgery are given hormonal treatment and psychologic guidance for some time preceding and following the surgical procedures.

The sex conversion operation for males is done in three stages: castration, removal of the penis, and plastic surgery to create an artificial vagina and external female genitalia. (The first recorded surgical attempt to create a vagina dates back to 1761 and was carried out on a female born without a vagina but with a normal uterus and ovaries.) Although the surgery ends male sexual function, sex relations as a female *are* possible, generally as soon as six to eight weeks after the operation.

It is not uncommon for the male transsexual also to request additional medical techniques to further feminize his appearance, including removal of beard and body hair by electrolysis, plastic facial operations (especially "nose bobs"), and breast enlargement, sometimes by augmentation mammaplasty. The younger surgical patients frequently express the desire to marry and adopt children. A number of them have married within six months after their sex-conversion surgery.

Female transsexuals, though even rarer in number than their male counterparts, are just as convinced that they are trapped in the wrong bodies. The majority request operations for the removal of their breasts, uterus, and ovaries. Most are aware that an artificial penis would not be erectile. There have, however, been surgical attempts to construct an artificial phallus and procedures to insert plastic testes into the folds of the labia. The younger patients usually want to marry and become husbands.

In the absence of proven genetic or endocrine causes for transsexualism, the popular current psychological theory places the blame on distorted family relationships that leave their imprint on a child before he or she is three years old. Greater knowledge in many areas of medicine and psychology is needed before all the causes of transsexualism are identified.

28

Sex in the Later Years

The so-called sexual revolution that started in the middle of the twentieth century is not confined to the population passing into puberty, but includes increasing millions of mature individuals, who are living longer and healthier lives. In nineteenth-century America only three percent of the population was sixty-five or older; today that percentage has tripled. In early 1965, there were an estimated 18 million people over sixty-five years of age in the United States, a number that is growing by approximately 1.4 million every year.

The whole area of human sexuality is currently being reassessed. Sexual activity in older people is being assessed for virtually the first time, for people have finally come to recognize the fact that sexuality is not limited to young people, but is a lifelong phenomenon. Depending upon such factors as personality, heredity, possible hormonal influences, and general health, sexual function is no more adversely affected by advancing years than any other body function. There are, however, racial and socioeconomic class distinctions in sexual behavior of older people: Negro men remain active longer than white men, and the poorer socioeconomic classes are active longer than the more prosperous socioeconomic classes.

Many different cultures fostered a repressive attitude toward sexuality. Intermarriages of people from varying backgrounds have led to freer attitudes, as has the new awareness of freedom that women have in all areas of life. Never in human history have so many women of all ages had such a positive attitude toward sexual gratification.

SEX AND THE OLDER WOMAN

Until recently, older women have not felt as free to talk about their sex lives as the "released" younger generation of women, and even physicians have been embarrassed to initiate a discussion about sex with women old enough to be grandmothers. Sam Levenson, the schoolteacher-philosopher television personality, reflecting on the reasons for the reluctance to discuss or even think about sexual behavior in older people, once said: "When I first found out how babies were born, I couldn't believe it! To think that my mother and father would do such a thing! . . . My father, maybe, but my mother—*never!*"

Few women today feel that the menopause means the end of sexual desire and fulfillment. Many women, relieved of the fear of becoming pregnant, develop revived—or even a new—interest in sex after the menopause. While sexual activity is less important to the average woman over fifty, women are capable of sexual response in very old age to a greater extent than men. However, there is such variation in frequency of sexual intercourse among older couples that it is almost impossible to generalize. Women's sexual activity naturally depends upon the sexual capacity of their husbands, and even when performance is inadequate or nonexistent, desire and interest tend to remain.

One of the major complaints of older women to physicians

is that their husbands do not show enough interest in them physically or emotionally. While the enjoyment and significance of the sex act may vary widely from woman to woman, there is a special need at this time of life for the simple affectionate gestures that pass between a husband and wife. For some women, these are enough to maintain a close and comfortable family relationship.

Of all the contributing factors to an older woman's sexual response, the most important are her own basic personality, her emotional response to her menopausal symptoms, her attitude toward her children and the end of her responsibilities toward them, and above all, the culmination of her feelings about her husband over the years.

SEX AND THE OLDER MAN

While women of today have the leisure, power, and means to search for eternal beauty, men throughout recorded history have searched for "The Fountain of Youth"—in reality, the pursuit of perpetual potency. Fierce attempts to improve and preserve their sex drive have led men to believe in and follow bizarre rituals of magic. Sexually stimulating effects have been ascribed to such foods as oysters, eggs, olives, celery, and wheat germ oil, and to such dangerous drugs as cantharides (crushed Spanish fly), which can produce toxic effects upon the urinary and gastrointestinal systems, and strychnine, a commonly used rat poison. Another common misconception is that alcoholic beverages are aphrodisiac, while the truth more often is that "when Bacchus enters, Aphrodite flies out the window."

Surveys have indicated that two thirds of men between the ages of fifty-five and seventy are sexually potent, and about one third remain so after the age of seventy. From age seventy to seventy-five, there is a distinct decline in activity, so that by seventy-five years of age, only fifty percent of men are still sexually active. Among potent older men, sexual activity is likely to continue if they are still married or, in the case of elderly bachelors or widowers, if by middle age they have had a regular sexual partner.

There are many influences affecting sexual adjustment in later life, including changing attitudes of each marital partner, family or business pressures, and illness and surgery—for example, heart disease and prostatectomy. Overwhelming fright frequently accompanying the early phase of a heart attack blots out all thoughts of sexual activity from a man's mind, but as he recovers and feels well again, he usually wants to resume activity in all areas of life. If he has been sexually active up until the time of his heart attack, his interest in sex will return. His physician will usually advise him when sexual relations may be safely resumed. Many a man facing a prostate operation is concerned about how the operation may effect his sexual ability. Recent studies have shown that most patients retain their potency after prostate surgery, the most important factor being the availability of a willing and able sexual partner.

The myths and misinformation revolving about the sexual interest and capacity of older people are being dispelled. Sexual interest does exist in most older men and many more older women than had previously been believed. A man who has been sexually active in his youth does not "burn out" as he gets older, but is more apt to maintain his sexual competency longer than men whose sexual activity had been more moderate. Not only do organic and environmental influences affect maintenance or loss of sexual potency in older men, but as in successful sexual encounters at all ages, psychological factors remain paramount.

Bibliography

Abortion and the Law, D. T. Smith, ed. Cleveland, Western Reserve University Press, 1967.

Adams, J. Q., *Chemistry and Therapy of Diseases of Pregnancy*. Springfield, Charles C Thomas, 1962.

Advances in Obstetrics and Gynecology, (Vol. I), S. L. Marcus and C. C. Marcus, eds. Baltimore, Williams and Wilkins Co., 1967.

Altman, H., "Respiratory Distress Syndrome of Newborn." *South African Medical Journal*, 39:746 (1965).

Alvarez, W. C., "Transsexuals." *Modern Medicine*, 35:80 (Jan. 16, 1967).

Ayd, F. J., Jr., "Contraceptives for Teenagers?" *Medical Science*, 18:20 (Sept. 1967).

———, "A New Non-Steroidal Ovulation Inducer: Clomiphene Citrate." *Medical Science*, 19:25 (Feb. 1968).

Barnes, C. G., *Medical Disorders in Obstetric Practice*. Philadelphia, F. A. Davis Co., 1965.

"Beaming in on Breast Cancer." *Medical World News*, 9:13 (Mar. 29, 1968).

Benjamin, H., "Clinical Aspects of Transsexualism in the Male and Female." *American Journal of Psychotherapy*, 18:458 (1964).

———, "Nature and Management of Transsexualism." *Western Journal of Surgery, Obstetrics, and Gynecology*, 72:105 (1964).

———, *The Transsexual Phenomenon*. New York, Julian Press, 1966.

Berland, T., "Cosmetic Surgery: What It Can and Cannot Do." *Today's Health*, 46:42 (June 1968).

Braz, J., *The Infertile Marriage*, trans. by A. J. Boerman. Haarlem, De Erven F. Bohn N.V., 1963.

Brown, R. S., "The 'Expanded' Rubella Syndrome." *Virginia Medical Monthly*, 94:232 (1967).

Bryant, R. D., and Overland, A. E., *Woodward and Gardner's Obstetric Management and Nursing*. Philadelphia, F. A. Davis Co., 1964.

The Case for Legalized Abortion, A. F. Guttmacher, ed. Berkeley, Diablo Press, 1967.

Cherry, S. H., "Amniotic Fluid Analysis As an Index of Fetal Health in Utero." *Medical Times*, 95:713 (1967).

Cherry, S. H., and Rosenfield, R. E., "Erythroblastosis Fetalis with Amniotic Fluid Studies and Intra-Uterine Fetal Transfusions: Clinical Evaluation and Management." *New York State Journal of Medicine*, 67:403 (1967).

Christenson, C. V., and Gagnon, J. H., "Sexual Behavior in a Group of Older Women." *Journal of Gerontology*, 20:351 (1965).

Cinberg, B. L., *For Women Only*. New York, Delacorte Press, Dial Press, 1964.

Clarkson, P., and Jeffs, J., "Modern Mammaplasty," *British Journal of Plastic Surgery*, 20:297 (1967).

Clinical Tuberculosis: Essentials of Diagnosis and Treatment, K. H. Pfuetze, and D. B. Radner, eds. Springfield, Charles C Thomas, 1966.

Cohen, M. M., Hirschhorn, K., and Frosch, W. A., "In Vivo and In Vitro Chromosomal Damage Induced by LSD-25." *New England Journal of Medicine*, 277:1043 (1967).

Connon, A. F., Hay, J. A. R., Kneebone, G. M., Jones, G. H., and Stentiford, H. B., "An Assessment of Intra-uterine Foetal Transfusion." *Medical Journal of Australia*, 2:93 (1967).

Crosse, V. M., *The Premature Baby and Other Babies with Low Birth Weight*, 6th ed. Boston, Little, Brown & Co., 1966.

Daly, M. J., "Sexual Attitudes in Menopausal and Postmenopausal Women." *Medical Aspects of Human Sexuality*, 2:48 (May 1968).

Davis, M. E., "Management of Infertility." *Journal of the American Medical Association*, 201:154 (1967).

―――, "Modern Management of Menopausal Patient." *Current Medical Digest*, 33:39 (1966).

De Savitsch, E., *Homosexuality, Transvestism and Change of Sex*. Springfield, Charles C Thomas, 1958.

Donald, I., and Abdulla, U., "Ultrasonics in Obstetrics and Gynaecology." *British Journal of Radiology*, 40:604 (1967).

Drill, V. A., *Oral Contraceptives*. New York, Blakiston Division, McGraw-Hill, 1966.

Drillien, C. M., *The Growth and Development of the Prematurely Born Infant*. Edinburgh, E. & S. Livingstone Ltd., 1964.

Drinan, R. F., "Abortion—3: Contemporary Protestant Thinking." *America*, 117:713 (1967).

Dudgeon, J. A., "Maternal Rubella and Its Effect on the Foetus." *Archives of Disease in Childhood*, 42:110 (1967).

Eastman, N. J., "Birth Weight and Intelligence." *Obstetrical and Gynecological Survey*, 22:61 (1967).

―――, "Induced Abortion and Contraception: A Consideration of Ethical Philosophy in Obstetrics." *Obstetrical and Gynecological Survey*, 22:3 (1967).

Eastman, N. J., and Hellman, L. M., *Williams Obstetrics*, 13th ed. New York, Appleton-Century-Crofts, Division of Meredith Publishing Co., 1966.

Eggen, R. R., *Chromosome Diagnostics in Clinical Medicine*. Springfield, Charles C Thomas, 1965.

"Estrogens During and After the Menopause." *The Medical Letter*, 7:54 (1965).

Feigenbaum, E. M., "A personal opinion on progress in care of the aged: Sexual attitudes in the elderly." *Geriatrics*, 22:42 (1967).

Feldman, H. J., and Reifenstein, E. C., Jr., "Oral Hormone Diagnostic Test for Early Pregnancy." *General Practitioner*, 33:78 (1966).

Finch, B. E., and Green, H., *Contraception through the Ages*. Springfield, Charles C Thomas, 1963.

Finkle, A. L., and Prian, D. V., "Sexual Potency in Elderly Men Before and After Prostatectomy." *Journal of the American Medical Association*, 196:139 (1966).

Fox, L. P., "Abortion Deaths in California." *American Journal of Obstetrics and Gynecology*, 98:648 (1967).

Fraser, A., *Heredity, Genes and Chromosomes*. New York, McGraw-Hill, 1966.

Frazer, J. G., *The New Golden Bough*, T. H. Gaster, ed. New York, Mentor Books, The New American Library, 1959.

Friedman, E. A., *Labor: Clinical Evaluation and Management*. New York, Appleton-Century-Crofts, Division of Meredith Publishing Co., 1967.

Gardner, E. J., *Principles of Genetics*. New York, John Wiley & Sons, Inc., 1964.

Gemzell, C., "Human Pituitary Gonadotropins in the Treatment of Sterility." *Fertility and Sterility*, 17:149 (1966).

Gershman, H., "Evolution of Gender Identity." *Bulletin of the New York Academy of Medicine*, 43:1000 (1967).

Gillespie, L., "Smoking and Low Birth Weight." *Clinical Obstetrics and Gynecology*, 7:658 (1964).

Glass, R. H., "Investigation of the Infertile Couple." *Connecticut Medicine*, 31:690 (1967).

Goldfarb, A. F., "Menopause—The Climacteric: Its Role in Aging." *Medical Science*, 18:48 (Feb. 1967).

Gorman, J. G., "Rh Immunoglobulin in Prevention of Hemolytic Disease of Newborn Child." *New York State Journal of Medicine*, 68:1270 (1968).

Greenblatt, R. B., "One-Pill-a-Month Contraceptive." *Fertility and Sterility*, 18:207 (1967).
———, "Progestational Agents in Clinical Practice." *Medical Science*, 18:37 (May 1967).
Guttmacher, A. F., *The Complete Book of Birth Control.* New York, Ballantine Books, 1963.
———, "The Contraceptive Problem." *Postgraduate Medicine*, 41:233 (1967).
Hagbard, L., *Pregnancy and Diabetes Mellitus.* Springfield, Charles C Thomas, 1961.
Hall, R. E., "Abortion in American Hospitals." *American Journal of Public Health*, 57:1933 (1967).
Hardin, G., "The History and Future of Birth Control." *Perspectives in Biology and Medicine*, 10:1 (1966).
Hardy, J. B., "Viral infection in pregnancy: A review." *American Journal of Obstetrics and Gynecology*, 93:1052 (1965).
Harter, C. L., and Beasley, J. D., "A Survey Concerning Induced Abortions in New Orleans." *American Journal of Public Health*, 57:1937 (1967).
Harthorne, J. W., Buckley, M. J., Grover, J. W., and Austen, W. G., "Valve Replacement During Pregnancy." *Annals of Internal Medicine*, 67:1032 (1967).
Hartman, C. G., Schoenfeld, C., and Copeland, E., "Individualism in the Semen Picture of Infertile Men." *Fertility and Sterility*, 15:231 (1964).
Hertz, R., "The role of steroid hormones in the etiology and pathogenesis of cancer." *American Journal of Obstetrics and Gynecology*, 98:1013 (1967).
Hertz, R., and Bailar, J. C., "Estrogen-Progestogen Combinations for Contraception." *Journal of the American Medical Association*, 198:136 (1966).
Heyns, O. S., *Abdominal Decompression.* Johannesburg, Witwatersrand University Press, 1963.
Hirt, N. B., "Sexual Difficulties After 50: The Psychiatrist's View." *Canadian Medical Association Journal*, 94:213 (1966).
Hitchcock, C. R., Hickok, D. F., Soucheray, J., Moulton, T.,

and Baker, R. C., "Thermography in Mass Screening for Occult Breast Cancer." *Journal of the American Medical Association*, 204:419 (1968).

Homosexuality, I. Bieber, ed. New York, Basic Books, 1962.

Hon, E. H., "Fetal Hazards of Labor." *Hospital Medicine*, 3:83 (May 1967).

———, *A Manual of Pregnancy Testing*. Boston, Little, Brown & Co., 1961.

Horger, E. O., III, Kellett, W. W., III, and Williamson, H. O., "Diabetes in Pregnancy: A Review of 143 Cases." *Obstetrics and Gynecology*, 30:46 (1967).

Hunt, W., and Beecham, C. T., "Current Concepts of Estrogen-Replacement Therapy." *Geisinger Medical Center Bulletin*, 18:119 (1966).

Hutt, M. L., and Gibby, R. G., *The Mentally Retarded Child: Development, Education and Treatment*. Boston, Allyn and Bacon, 1965.

Iorio, J., *Principles of Obstetrics and Gynecology for Nurses*. St. Louis, C. V. Mosby Co., 1967.

Irwin, T., "High-Risk Care Saves Lives and Minds." *Today's Health*, 46:42 (Jan. 1968).

Israel, S. L., *Diagnosis and Treatment of Menstrual Disorders and Sterility*, 5th ed. New York, Hoeber Medical Division, Harper & Row, 1967.

Israel, S. L., and Rubin, I., "*SIECUS Study Guide No. 6: Sexual Relations During Pregnancy and the Post-Delivery Period*." Sex Information and Education Council of the U.S., 1967.

Jackson, H., *Antifertility Compounds in the Male and Female*. Springfield, Charles C Thomas, 1966.

Jacobson, W. E., "Cancer of the breast." *Modern Medicine*, 36:61 (Jan. 1, 1968).

Jakobovits, I., *Jewish Medical Ethics*. New York, Bloch Publishing Co., 1962.

Jones, G. S., "Prognosis for the Infertile Couple." *Obstetrical and Gynecological Survey*, 20:646 (1965).

Jones, H. W., Jr., Schirmer, H. K. A., and Hoopes, J. E., "A

BIBLIOGRAPHY

sex conversion operation for males with transsexualism." *American Journal of Obstetrics and Gynecology,* 100:101 (1968).

Karmody, C. S., "Subclinical Maternal Rubella and Congenital Deafness." *New England Journal of Medicine,* 278:809 (1968).

Kase, N., "Medical Induction of Ovulation in Anovulatory Infertility." *Connecticut Medicine,* 31:695 (1967).

Kaufman, S. A., *The Ageless Woman.* Englewood Cliffs, Prentice-Hall, Inc., 1967.

Kinch, R. A. H., "Sexual Difficulties After 50: The Gynecologist's View." *Canadian Medical Association Journal,* 94:211 (1966).

Kleegman, S. J., "Therapeutic Donor Insemination." *Connecticut Medicine,* 31:705 (1967).

Kleegman, S. J., and Kaufman, S. A., *Infertility in Women.* Philadelphia, F. A. Davis Co., 1966.

Kourides, I. A., "Freedom of Birth: Methods of Population Control Today." *Medical Science,* 18:25 (Aug. 1967).

Krieg, A. F., and Henry, J. B., "Pregnancy Tests, Part 2." *Postgraduate Medicine,* 42:A-48 (Sept. 1967).

Lader, L., *Abortion.* New York, Bobbs-Merrill Co., 1966.

Lash, A. F., "Review of More than 20 Years' Experience with the Incompetent Internal Os of the Cervix." *Fertility and Sterility,* 15:254 (1964).

Lenz, W., "Malformations Caused by Drugs in Pregnancy." *American Journal of Diseases of Children,* 112:99 (1966).

Lewison, E. F., "Breast Cancer." *Maryland State Medical Journal,* 15:39 (1966).

Litton, C., "Follow-Up Study of Chemosurgery." *Southern Medical Journal,* 59:1007 (1966).

Lloyd, T. S., Jr., "Obstetrical Use of the Ultrasonic Doppler Instrument." *Journal of the American Medical Association,* 204:105 (1968).

Loraine, J. A., and Bell, E. T., *Hormone Assays and Their Clinical Application.* Edinburgh, E. & S. Livingstone Ltd., 1966.

Lucey, J. F., "The Newborn Special Care Unit in the Community Hospital Setting." *Hospital Practice*, 3:27 (Jan. 1968).

Lytton, B., and Mroueh, A., "Treatment of Oligospermia with Urinary Human Menopausal Gonadotrophin: A Preliminary Report." *Fertility and Sterility*, 17:696 (1966).

McEwen, D. C., "Reconstructive Tubal Surgery." *Fertility and Sterility*, 17:39 (1966).

McKendry, J. B. J., and Bailey, J. D., *Paediatric Problems in General Practice: The New-Born.*" Springfield, Charles C Thomas, 1965.

McKusick, V. A., "Chromosomes, Genes and Families," in *Birth Defects*, M. Fishbein, ed. Philadelphia, J. B. Lippincott Co., 1963.

———, *Heritable disorders of connective tissue.* St. Louis, C. V. Mosby Co., 1966.

———, *Human Genetics.* Englewood Cliffs, Prentice-Hall, Inc., 1964.

Mandelbaum, B., Pontarelli, D. A., and Brushenko, A., "Amnioscopy for prenatal transfusion." *American Journal of Obstetrics and Gynecology*, 98:1140 (1967).

Manual of Contraceptive Practice, M. S. Calderone, ed. Baltimore, Williams and Wilkins Co., 1964.

Marchant, D. J., Bardawil, W. A., Mitchell, G. W., Jr., and Carey, E., "Observations on the Behavior of Skin Homografts in Human Pregnancy." *Fertility and Sterility*, 15:272 (1964).

Masland, R. L., "Tracking Down the Causes of Birth Defects." *Today's Health*, 44:60 (Aug. 1966).

Masters, W. H., and Johnson, V. E., *Human Sexual Response.* Boston, Little, Brown & Co., 1966.

Medical, Surgical, and Gynecologic Complications of Pregnancy, J. J. Rovinsky and A. F. Guttmacher, eds. Baltimore, Williams and Wilkins Co., 1965.

Mroueh, A., "Diagnosis and Treatment of Male Infertility." *Connecticut Medicine*, 31:698 (1967).

Novak, E. R., "Replacement Therapy of the Menopause." *Johns Hopkins Medical Journal*, 120:408 (1967).
Novak, E. R., and Jones, G. S., *Novak's Textbook of Gynecology*, 6th ed. Baltimore, Williams and Wilkins Co., 1961.
Novak, E. R., and Woodruff, J. D., *Gynecologic and Obstetric Pathology With Clinical and Endocrine Relations*. Philadelphia, W. B. Saunders Co., 1962.
Oken, D. E., "Chronic renal diseases and pregnancy: A review." *American Journal of Obstetrics and Gynecology*, 94:1023 (1966).
Olson, L. E., "Immunologic Studies in Infertility." *Connecticut Medicine*, 31:703 (1967).
Page, I. H., "The malforming (teratogenic) effect of a viral infection." *Modern Medicine*, 36:69 (May 6, 1968).
Parks, J., "Care of the Postmenopausal Patient." *Postgraduate Medicine*, 42:275 (1967).
Peberdy, G., "Sex and Its Problems: Sexual Adjustment at the Climacteric." *The Practitioner*, 199:564 (1967).
Pincus, G., *The Control of Fertility*. New York, Academic Press, 1965.
Queenan, J. T., *Modern Management of the Rh Problem*. New York, Hoeber Medical Division, Harper & Row, 1967.
Raphael, M. J., Gordon, H., and Schiff, D., "Radiological aspects of intra-uterine blood transfusion." *British Journal of Radiology*, 40:520 (1967).
Rawls, W. E., Desmyter, J., and Melnick, J. L., "Serologic Diagnosis and Fetal Involvement in Maternal Rubella—Criteria for Abortion." *Journal of the American Medical Association*, 203:111 (1968).
Reed, S. C., *Counseling In Medical Genetics*. Philadelphia, W. B. Saunders Co., 1963.
Rhoades, F. P., "Minimizing the Menopause." *Journal of The American Geriatrics Society*, 15:346 (1967).
Roberts, J. A. F., *An Introduction to Medical Genetics*. New York, Oxford University Press, 1967.
Robinson, D., Rock, J., and Menkin, M. F., "Control of

Human Spermatogenesis by Induced Changes of Intrascrotal Temperature." *Journal of the American Medical Association*, 204:80 (1968).

Robinson, H. B., and Robinson, N. M., *The Mentally Retarded Child: A Psychological Approach*. New York, McGraw-Hill, 1965.

Roemer, R., "Abortion Law: The Approaches of Different Nations." *American Journal of Public Health*, 57:1906 (1967).

Roland, M., "The Infertile Couple." *Medical Times*, 95:71 (1967).

"Rubella Study Puts Defect Rate at Almost 90%." *Medical World News*, 8:35 (Sept. 29, 1967).

Schwartz, R. W., "Clinical Considerations of Rubella in Pregnancy." *New York State Journal of Medicine*, 68:392 (1968).

Shapiro, S., Strax, P., and Venet, L., "Periodic Breast Cancer Screening." *Archives of Environmental Health*, 15:547 (1967).

Sherman, J. K., "Research on Frozen Human Semen: Past, Present, and Future." *Fertility and Sterility*, 15:485 (1964).

Siegel, M., Fuerst, H. T., and Duggan, W., "Rubella in Mother and Congenital Cataracts in Child." *Journal of the American Medical Association*, 203:116 (1968).

Silverman, W. A., and Sinclair, J. C., "Current Concepts: Infants of Low Birth Weight." *New England Journal of Medicine*, 274:448 (1966).

Singer, A., Thomas, R., and Spector, B., "An Automatic System for the Measurement and Recording of Basal Temperature in the Human Female." *Fertility and Sterility*, 15:44 (1964).

Sites, J. G., and Jacobson, C. B., "Genetic Counseling in Obstetrics and Gynecology." *Annals of The New York Academy of Sciences*, 142:768 (1967).

Stallworthy, J., and Bourne, G., *Recent Advances in Obstetrics and Gynaecology*. Boston, Little, Brown & Co., 1966.

"Statistics On Cancer," *Ca* (Adapted from *1967 Cancer Facts and Figures*, American Cancer Society), 17:34 (1967).

Stevenson, C. S., "Myomectomy for Improvement of Fertility." *Fertility and Sterility*, 15:367 (1964).

Stevenson, S. S., "Recent Advances in the Management of the Rh-Incompatible Pregnancy." *Bulletin of the New York Academy of Medicine*, 42:455 (1966).

Stewart, B. H., "The Infertile Male: A Diagnostic Approach." *Fertility and Sterility*, 17:783 (1966).

Stoller, R. J., " 'It's Only a Phase': Femininity in Boys." *Journal of the American Medical Association*, 201:98 (1967).

———, "The Treatment of Transvestism and Transsexualism." *Current Psychiatric Therapies*, 6:92 (1966).

Strassmann, E. O., "Fertility and Unification of Double Uterus." *Fertility and Sterility*, 17:165 (1966).

Stuart-Harris, C. H., *Influenza*. Baltimore, Williams and Wilkins Co., 1965.

Swartz, D., "Sexual Difficulties After 50: The Urologist's View." *Canadian Medical Association Journal*, 94:208 (1966).

Taylor, B. W., Litin, E. M., and Litzow, T. J., "Psychiatric Considerations in Cosmetic Surgery." *Mayo Clinic Proceedings*, 41:608 (1966).

Taylor, E. S., *Beck's Obstetrical Practice*, 8th ed. Baltimore, Williams and Wilkins Co., 1966.

Taylor, H. C., "Evaluation of Recent Developments in Contraceptive Technology." *American Journal of Public Health* (supplement), 56:74 (1966).

"Tests for Pregnancy." *British Medical Journal*, 3:448 (1967).

Theologides, A., and Kennedy, B. J., "Therapeutic management of advanced female breast cancer." *Modern Medicine*, 35:74 (Jan. 1, 1967).

Thompson, M. W., "Genetic Counseling in Clinical Pediatrics: What to Do with Inquiries about Heritable Disorders." *Clinical Pediatrics*, 6:199 (1967).

Tietze, C., "Abortion in Europe." *American Journal of Public Health*, 57:1923 (1967).
Todays' *Health Guide*, W. W. Bauer, ed. Chicago, American Medical Association, 1965.
Töndury, G., "Aetiological Factors in Human Malformation." *Triangle*, 7:90 (1965).
Vulliamy, D. G., *The Newborn Child*. Boston, Little, Brown & Co., 1967.
Willey, R. D., and Waite, K. B., *The Mentally Retarded Child: Identification, Acceptance, and Curriculum*. Springfield, Charles C Thomas, 1964.
Winchester, J. H., "Rescuing Newborns with Minisurgery." *Today's Health*, 46:52 (Jan. 1968).
Yerushalmy, J., "The Low-Birthweight Baby." *Hospital Practice*, 3:62 (May 1968).
Zellweger, H., "Genetic counseling in clinical medicine." *Modern Medicine*, 35:40 (Oct. 9, 1967).

Index

ABO incompatibility, 117–118, 171, 187
"A-Z" pregnancy test, 88
Abortion, 53–84
   ancient civilizations and, 55–56
   Catholic viewpoint, 56, 57–58
   criminal, deaths from, 65, 70–71, 81–82
   "D and C" hospital method, 80
   dangers of "do-it-yourself," 81–82
   diabetes and, 94–95
   drug-induced, 81
   future of, 82–84
   German measles and, 60, 80
   habitual, 190
   heart disease and, 93–94
   hospital, 58, 79–81
   illegal, 65, 70, 74, 81
   incest and, 75–76
   induced, 55–84
   injected hypertonic glucose or salt solution, 80–81, 93
   Jewish viewpoint, 59–60
   "la sonda," 70–71
   laws in foreign countries, 65–71, 73–74, 76–77, 83
   laws in the U.S., 73–77, 83–84
   Model Penal Code, 75, 76, 84
   Protestant viewpoint, 60–63
   public health problem, 74
   quickening and, 74
   rape and, 75, 76–77
   Roman Catholic viewpoint, 56, 57–58
   rubella (German measles) and, 60, 80
   spontaneous, 95, 169, 171, 187
   teen-age, incidence of, 47
   thalidomide and, 139–140
   therapeutic, 58, 60, 61, 62, 79–84, 94, 95
   threatened, 106–107
   tuberculosis and, 60, 70, 95–96
   "vacuum" method, 81
Abrasive facial skin treatments, 210
Abstinence:
   in infertility, 170, 187
   during pregnancy, 105–107

INDEX

Acne, 19, 210
Adrenal glands, 170, 184
Aerosol foam, see Foam
Alcohol and potency, 217
Allen, Dr. F. H., 114
Amenorrhea, 169
American Cancer Society, 201
American Law Institute, 75, 77
　See also Abortion
Aminopterin, 80, 139
Amniocentesis, 115, 116, 117
Amniography, 116
Amnion, 115
Amnioscopy, 116, 146
Amniotic fluid, examination of, 115–117
Amniotic sac, 115
Androgens, 204
Animal husbandry, 4, 51, 166, 191
Apgar, Dr. Virginia, 147–148
Apgar test for newborns, 147–148
Aphrodisiacs, 217
Aphrodite, 217
Aristotle, 56, 59
Artificial insemination, 166, 191–193
Aschheim-Zondek pregnancy test, 88
Association for Voluntary Sterilization, 41
Augmentation mammaplasty, 211
Azoospermia, 175

"Baby blues," 106
Bacchus, 217
Bacteriuria, during pregnancy, 97
Bag of waters, see Membranes, fetal
Bags under the eyes, plastic surgery for, 209
Basal body temperature, see Temperature, basal body
"Being careful," see Withdrawal
Besant, Mrs. Annie, 6
Biopsy:
　endometrial, 182, 190
　testicular, 173

Birnberg bow, 24
Birth control, 3–52
　"accidents" and abortion, 82
　"best" method, 11–13
　future of, 51–52
　history of, 3–9
　infanticide, 4
　intrauterine devices (IUD), 5, 12, 23–26
　minors and, 47–49
　movement, 6
　oral contraceptives (The Pill), 12, 15–21
　other methods, effectiveness of, 27–34, 35–40
　sterilization, female and male, 41–45
　See also Contraceptives
Birth control pills, see Contraceptives
Birth defects, 121–142
　diseases causing, 140–142
　drugs causing, 81, 139–140
　early treatment of, 144–145, 150–154
　genetic counseling services in the U.S. for prevention of, 128–139
　genetic counselor and, 122–123, 127
　heredity and, 121, 122–127
　radiation and, 81, 121
Bladder infections, during pregnancy, 96
"Bleeder's disease," 126
Bleeding, breakthrough, 18, 20
Blepharoplasty, 209
Bones, brittle, 200
Boswell, James, 5
Bourne v. the Crown, 76–77
　See also Abortion
Brain damage, see Mental retardation
Breakthrough bleeding, 18, 20
Breast:
　breastfeeding and conception, 40

Breast (*continued*)
  cancer of, diagnosis and treatment, 201-204
  plastic surgery of, 210-211
Breast surgery:
  for cancer, 203-204
  for cosmetic reasons, 210-211

Caesarean section, 94, 95, 113, 114, 150
Calderone, Dr. Mary S., 13
Cancer detection tests:
  breast, 202-203
  cervix and uterus, 204-205
Cantharides (Spanish fly), 217
Casanova, 5
Castor oil, 102
Castration:
  female, 43, 204
  male, 213
Cataracts, congenital, 140-141
Catholic Church:
  Canon Law, 57, 58
  infertility diagnosis and, 175
  rhythm technique, 37-38
  viewpoint on abortion, 56, 57-58, 63, 73
Cervical cap, 6, 29-30
  See also Contraceptives
Cervical mucus, *see* Cervix
Cervimetry, during labor, 102
Cervix:
  cancer of, 21, 204-205
  cap, cervical, 6, 29-30
  closed, 169, 187
  dilatation of, 23, 80, 102
  endocervicitis, 187
  incompetent, 149, 187-188
  infertility and, 169-170, 185-188
  labor and, 99, 102
  mucus, cervical, 17, 51, 182-183, 186, 187
  polyps of, 187
"Change of life," 198
  See also Menopause
Chemabrasion, 210

Chemosurgery, 210
Chin, plastic surgery of, 208
Chlormadinone (The Minipill), 51
Chorion, 88, 115
Chromosomes, 123-125
Clarke, Dr. Cyril, 118
Cleft lip, 125, 151-152, 208
Cleft palate, 125, 208
Climacteric, 198
  See also Menopause
Climax, *see* Orgasm
Clomiphene citrate, 184-185
Clubfoot, 121, 125, 151
Cobalt therapy, 204
Coitus, *see* Sexual relations
Coitus incompletus, *see* Withdrawal
Coitus interruptus, *see* Withdrawal
Coitus reservatus, *see* Withdrawal
Coitus saxonicus, *see* Withdrawal
Color blindness, 121
"Combined" birth control methods, 32
Combined contraceptive pill, 17
  See also Contraceptives
Complex Marriage, 7
Comstock, Anthony, 7
Comstock Law, 7, 8
Conception, 4, 16-17
Condom, 30-32
  failure of, 31-32
  historical references to, 5
  infertility, use in, 170, 187
  plastic, 175
  premature ejaculation, use in, 31
  rubber, 5, 31, 175
  skin, 5, 31
Congenital heart defects:
  fetal, and maternal rubella, 141
  maternal, in pregnancy, 94
  newborn, minisurgery for, 151-153
Congenital malformations, *see* Birth Defects

INDEX

Contraceptives, 3–52
  ancient practices, 4–5
  cervical cap, 6, 29–30
  "combined" methods, 32
  condom, 5, 30–32, 170, 175, 187
  cream, vaginal, 28, 30, 32, 36, 38
  diaphragm, vaginal, 6, 8, 12, 27–29, 32
  douche, vaginal, 6, 28, 36, 38, 39, 40
  female sterilization, 41–44, 45
  foam, aerosol, 36–37
  intrauterine devices (IUD), 5, 12, 23–26
  jelly, vaginal, 4, 28, 30, 32, 36, 38
  legislation, Comstock Law, 7, 8
  male sterilization, 41, 44–45
  for minors, 47–49
  oral (The Pill), 15–21
  rhythm, 37–38
  sponge and foam, 38–39
  sponge with household spermatocides, 39
  suppositories, vaginal, 4, 36
  tampons with household spermatocides, 39
  vaginal sponge, 6, 38–39
  withdrawal, 6, 7, 32–34, 75
  See also Birth control
Coombs test, 113, 114
Cord, umbilical, 93, 113, 114, 116, 149, 158
Coronary disease, *see* Heart disease
Cosmetic surgery, 207–213
  breasts, 210–211
  chin, 208
  ear, 210
  eyelids, 209
  face-lift, 209
  fat deposits, 211–212
  jaw, 211
  nose, 208–209
  sex transformation, 212–213
Counseling, genetic, 122–123, 127, 128–139

Cream, vaginal, 28, 30, 32, 36, 38
  See also Contraceptives
Criminal abortion, *see* Abortion
Culdoscope, 43, 189
Culdoscopy, 189
Curettage, 80
  See also Uterus
Curette, 80
Cystitis, during pregnancy, 96–97

"D and C," 80
  See also Abortion *and* Uterus
DNA, 176
Deafness, 60, 139, 141
Defects, congenital, *see* Birth defects
Depression, 19, 106, 199
Dermabrasion, 210
Deviated septum, 208
Diabetes, 126, 169
  pregnancy and, 94–95, 102, 146, 149, 150
Diamond, Dr. L. K., 114
Diaphragm, vaginal, 6, 8, 12, 27–29, 37
  See also Contraceptives
Dickinson, Dr. Robert L., 191
Dilatation of the cervix:
  Grafenberg ring and, 23
  during labor, 99, 102
  for therapeutic abortion, 80
Dislocation of the hip, congenital, 121, 125
Diuretics, 20, 92, 94
Donor insemination, 191–193
Double uterus, 170, 190, 191
  See also Uterus
Douche, vaginal, 6, 28, 36, 38, 39, 40
  See also Contraceptives
Down's syndrome (mongolism), 121, 126

Ear, plastic surgery of, 210
Ebers Papyrus, 4, 94

INDEX

Ectopic pregnancy (tubal), 58, 81
Egg, see Follicle, human egg
Egypt, ancient, 4, 87, 94, 207
Ejaculation:
  abnormalities of, 168–169
  ducts, ejaculatory, 44, 174
  infertility diagnosis and, 174–175
  premature, 31, 33, 168, 177
  after vasectomy, 44
  withdrawal and, 32–34
Electrocardiogram, fetal, 93
Ellenborough Act, 74
Embolism, see Pulmonary embolism
Embryo, 115, 123, 139, 141
Embryotomy, 59, 60
Endocervicitis, 187
Endocervix, 183
Endometriosis, 169
Endometrium, 181
  biopsy of, 182, 190
  effect of The Pill on, 17
  polyps of, 190
Epididymis, 168, 174
Epilepsy, 125
Erection, 32, 44
Erythroblastosis fetalis, see Rh disease
Estrogens:
  breast cancer and, 201, 204
  deficiency of, 187, 199–200
  heart disease and, 199
  infertility and, 187
  menopause and, 198–200
  menstrual cycle and, 180–181
  The Pill, 17
  replacement therapy, 199–200
Exchange transfusion, 114
"Extrauterine life," 145
Eyelids, plastic surgery of, 209

FSH (follicle-stimulating hormone), 180
Face-lift, 209

Fallopian tubes:
  ectopic pregnancy in, 58, 81
  effect of IUD on, 24
  fertility and, 175
  infertility and, 169, 188–190
  insufflation of, 43, 188
  reversal of sterilization, 43
  surgical removal of, 42–43
  X-ray of, 188–189
Fallopius, 5
"False" negative, in pregnancy test, 89
"False" positive, in pregnancy test, 89
Female infertility, 165–167
  causes of, 169–170
  diagnosis and treatment of, 179–183
  influence of age on, 167–168
  unexplained, 170–171
Female sterilization, 41–44, 45
Fern test, for ovulation, 182, 185, 187
Fertilization, 16, 17, 33, 173, 179, 191–193
Fetal blood sampling, 146–147
Fetal electrocardiogram, 93
Fetal membranes, see Membranes, fetal
Fetal surgery, 153–154
Fetus:
  surgery on, 153–154
  transition to newborn, 142–152
  treatment for, in Rh disease, 117
Fibroid tumors, 170, 190, 191
  See also Uterus
Finkbine, Mrs. Sherri, 140
Finn, Dr. Ronald, 118
Flushes, hot, 19, 198, 199
Foam:
  aerosol, 36–37
  sponge and, 38–39
  vaginal tablets for, 36–37
  See also Contraceptives
Follicle, human egg, 16, 180
  See also Ovaries

INDEX

Foreskin, 31
"Fountain of Youth," 217
Freda, Dr. Vincent, 118
Friedman pregnancy test, 88
Frigidity and withdrawal, 34

Galactosemia, 127, 158, 160
Galli-Mainini pregnancy test, 89
Gamma globulin for Rh disease, 118
  See also Rh disease
Gender identity, 212
Gender Identity Clinic, 212–213
Genes, 122-125
  dominant, 124
  recessive, 124, 159, 160
  sex-linked, 124–125
Genetic counseling, 122–123, 127
  services in the U.S., 128–139
Genetic disorders, 125–127
  See also Birth defects
German measles, *see* Rubella
Glaucoma, from maternal rubella, 141
Gonad, *see* Ovaries *and* Testes
Gonadotrophins, human:
  chorionic, 87–90, 185
  menopausal, 177, 185
  pituitary, 174, 185
Gonorrhea, *see* Venereal disease
Gorman, Dr. John G., 118
Graafian follicle, *see* Follicle, human egg
Grafenberg ring, 23
Greece, ancient, 56
Guttmacher, Dr. Alan F., 5

HCG (human chorionic gonadotrophin), 87–90, 185
HMG (human menopausal gonadotrophin), 177, 185
HMG-HCG therapy, for infertility, 185
Habitual abortion, *see* Abortion
Hall-Stone steel ring, 24

Hardin, Garrett, Ph.D., 82–83, 84
Harelip, 125, 151–152, 208
Hartnup disease, 160
Heart attacks, sexual activity after, 218
Heart disease:
  estrogens and, 199
  in pregnancy, 93–94
Hemophilia, 126
Hemorrhage:
  before delivery, 150, 158
  from self-induced abortion, 70, 81–82
Heredity:
  disease and, 121, 122, 124–127
  Mendelian theory of, 123, 124
  See also Birth defects
High blood pressure, in pregnancy, 91–92, 149
Hip, congenital dislocation of, 121, 125
Hippocrates, 56, 125, 166
Hogben pregnancy test, 89
Homosexuality, 212
Hormones, female, *see* Estrogens, HCG, HMG *and* Progesterone
Hormones, male, *see* Androgens *and* Testosterone
Hot flushes, 19, 198, 199
Human chorionic gonadotrophin (HCG), 87–90, 185
Human menopausal gonadotrophin (HMG), 177, 185
Human pituitary gonadotrophins, 174, 177, 181, 185
Hunter, Dr. John, 191
Hyaline membrane disease, 151
Hyams sterilization technique, 43
Hydrocephalus, 121
Hydrotubation, 189
Hymen, intact:
  diaphragm fitted for, 28
  pregnancy and, 33
Hyperbaric chamber, 152
Hypnosis and childbirth, 101

INDEX

Hypophysectomy, 204
Hypothyroidism, 177
Hysterectomy, 43, 58
Hysterography, 190
Hysterosalpingography, 188–189
Hysterotomy, 80

IUD, see Intrauterine devices
Illegitimacy, 47
Immunoglobulin, Rh, 118–119
Immunological pregnancy test, 89–90
Impotence, 34, 177, 217–218
Inborn errors of metabolism, 158–161
Incest and abortion, 75–76
   See also Abortion
Induction of labor, see Labor
Infant:
   low birth weight, 148–150
   mortality, 146, 149, 150, 151
   premature, 122, 148–153, 158
   See also Newborn child
Infanticide, 4
   See also Birth control
Infections:
   abortion, self-induced, and, 70–71, 80–81
   bladder, during pregnancy, 96
   infertility and, 169
   kidney, during pregnancy, 96
   venereal, 5, 31, 47–48, 169
Infertility, 3
   female, 165–168, 169–171, 179–193
   male, 166, 168–169, 173–178
   unexplained, 170–171
Influenza and pregnancy, 97, 142
Insemination, artificial, 166, 191–193
Intensive care units:
   for sick and premature newborns, 150
   for women in labor, 92
Intercourse, see Sexual relations
Intrauterine devices, 5, 12, 23–26
   See also Contraceptives

Intrauterine pressure tracing, during labor, 93
Intrauterine transfusion, 117
Itard, Dr. Jean, 155–156

Jakobovits, Rabbi Immanuel, 59–60
Jaundice in infants, causes of: 112, 118, 141, 160
Jaw, plastic surgery of, 211
Jelly, vaginal, 4, 28, 30, 32, 36
   See also Contraceptives
Jewish viewpoint on abortion, 59–60
Johns Hopkins Hospital, 212
Johnson, Mrs. Virginia, 29, 106
Jones, Dr. A. R., 114
Jorgensen, Christine, 212

Karezza, see Withdrawal
Kidney:
   damage from self-induced abortion, 82
   embryonic, 174
   infections during pregnancy, 96
Kinsey, Dr. Alfred C., 33
Klinefelter's syndrome, 127
Kupperman pregnancy test, 88

LH (luteinizing hormone), 180
LSD, damage to fetus from, 140
Labia, 33, 213
Labor:
   abdominal decompression during, 101
   control of, 99–102
   hypnosis during, 101
   induction of, 95, 101–102, 113, 114
   monitoring, 93
   "natural" childbirth, 101
   stages of, 99
Lader, Lawrence, 74
Landsteiner, Dr. Karl, 111

INDEX

"La sonda," 70–71
  See also Abortion
van Leeuwenhoek, Anton, 174–175
Life expectancy, 197
Liley, Dr. A. W., 117
Lippes loop, 24
Low birth weight infant, 148–150

Madlener sterilization technique, 42
Maimonides, 59
Male contraceptive pill, 52
Male fertility and cold showers, 178
Male genitourinary tract, 44
Male infertility, 166
  causes of, 168–169
  diagnosis and treatment of, 173–178
  unexplained, 170–171
Male sterilization, 41, 44–45
Malthus, Thomas Robert, 6, 9
Mammaplasty:
  augmentation, 211
  reduction, 211
Mammography, 202
Mantegazza, Paolo, 192, 193
Maple-syrup urine disease, 161
Marco-Nash plastic "harp," 24
Margulies spiral, 24
Mastectomy, 203–204
Masters, Dr. William H., 29, 106
Masturbation and sperm counts, 175
Maternal mortality, 65–66, 91, 96
Membranes, fetal, 9, 102, 107
Menarche, 180
Mendel, Gregor, 123
Mendelian laws of heredity, 123, 124
Menopause, 181, 197–200
  estrogen replacement therapy for, 199–200
  The Pill and, 17
  sex after, 215–217
  symptoms of, 198–200

Menoplasty, 208
Menstruation, 3
  amenorrhea, 169
  beginning of, 180
  end of, 181, 197–199
  induction of, after delivery, 103
  infertility problems and, 170
  menstrual cycle, 180–181
  The Pill and, 18
Mental retardation, causes of:
  galactosemia, 158, 160
  Hartnup syndrome, 160
  maple-sugar urine disease, 161
  maternal rubella, 141
  meningitis, 158
  PKU (phenylketonuria), 158, 159–160
  Rh disease, 112, 158
  Wilson's disease, 160
Metabolism, inborn errors of, 158–161
Metastasis, 204
Methotrexate, 81
Metroplasty, 191
Meyer, Dr. Harry M., Jr., 141
Miller-Kurzrock test (semen penetration), 186
Minipill, The, 51
Minisurgery, 151–153
Minors:
  abortion in, 47
  contraceptives for, 47–49
Miscarriage, 4, 107, 121, 122, 124
  See also Abortion, spontaneous
Model Penal Code, 75, 76, 84
  See also Abortion
Mongolism (Down's syndrome), 121, 126
"Morning-after pill," 52, 84
Mortality rates:
  infant, 146, 149, 150, 151
  maternal, 65–66, 91, 96
Multiple pregnancy, 93, 149
Myomata, 191
Myomectomy, 191
Myometrium, 181

INDEX

Nash plastic "earring" device, 24
National Council on Illegitimacy, 47
National Foundation-March of Dimes, 127
"Natural" childbirth, 101
Newborn child:
 intensive care unit for, 150
 low birth weight infant, 148–150
 minisurgery for, 151–153
 premature, 122, 148–151, 158
 transition from fetus, 145–154
Nose, plastic surgery of, 208
Noyes, John Humphrey, 7

Oettinger, Katherine B., 48
Oligospermia, 175
Onanism, see Withdrawal
Oneida community, 7
Oophorectomy, 43, 204
Open-heart surgery:
 during pregnancy, 94
 on newborns, 151–152
Oral contraceptives, 15–21
 See also Birth control
Oregon Regional Primate Research Center, 153
Orgasm, 32, 33, 174, 175
Osteoporosis, 200
Otoplasty, 210
Ova, ovum, 16, 169, 171, 193
 See also Ovaries
Ovaries:
 development and function of, 16–17, 180–181
 egg follicle within, 16, 180
 infertility and, 182–185
 menopause and, 198
 oocytes (immature egg cells), 180, 185
 ova (mature egg cells), 16, 169, 171, 193
 removal of, 43, 204
 transplantation of tissue from, 185

Ovulation, 17, 37–38
 induction of, 184–185
 normal, 180–181
 tests to determine, 182–183
Oxytocin, 102

PKU (phenylketonuria), 140, 158, 159–160
Palate, cleft, 125, 208
Panculdoscope, 189
Pap test, 204–205
Papanicolaou, Dr. George N., 204
 See also Pap test
Paraffin injections into breasts, 211
Parkman, Dr. Paul D., 142
Pelvimetry, 100
Penis:
 artificial, 213
 condom for, 5, 30–32, 170, 187
 ejaculation and, 174
 fetal, 116
 surgical removal of, 213
 withdrawal, 6, 7, 32–34
Pessary, 191
Phallus, see Penis
Phenylketonuria (PKU), 127, 158, 159–160
Pill, The, 15–21, 166, 184
Pincus, Dr. Gregory, 15, 17
Pinel, Dr. Philippe, 155
Pituitary gland, 16, 170, 184, 204, 209
Pituitary gonadotrophic hormones, 174, 177, 181, 185
Placenta, 87, 92, 93, 99, 102, 148, 158
Placentography, 92
Planned Parenthood Federation of America, 8
Plastic surgery, see Cosmetic surgery
Plato, 56
Polio and pregnancy, 97, 142
Pollack, Dr. William, 118
Polyps:
 cervical, 187
 endometrial, 190

Pomeroy sterilization technique, 42
Population trends, 9, 16, 215
Postcoital test (Sims-Huhner), 186
Postmaturity, 122, 146
Potency, sexual:
  alcohol and, 217
  infertility and, 173
  older men and, 215–216, 217–218
  unimpaired after vasectomy, 44–45
Pregnancy:
  ectopic (tubal), 58, 81
  fetal electrocardiogram, 93
  multiple, diagnosing, 93
  safer, 91–97
  sexual relations during and after, 105–107
  tests for, 87–90
  ultrasound waves and, 93
Premature ejaculation, 31, 33, 168, 177
Premature infant, 122, 148–153, 158
Prenatal care, 91–97, 158–159
Progesterone:
  infertility and, 190–191
  menstrual cycle and, 180–181
  The Pill, 17
Prostate gland, 174
  surgery, sexual activity after, 218
Protestant viewpoint on abortion, 60–63
Puberty, 16, 174, 180, 197
Pulmonary embolism:
  self-induced abortion and, 82
  The Pill and, 21
Pyelitis, during pregnancy, 96–97
Pyelonephritis, during pregnancy, 96–97, 102
Pythagoreans, 56
Pyuria, during pregnancy, 97

Quinine, 102, 139

Radical mastectomy, 203–204
Radiotherapy, for breast cancer, 204
Rape and abortion, 75, 76–77
  See also Abortion
Reduction mammaplasty, 211
Renaissance, 31, 207
Respiratory distress syndrome, 150–151
Retardation, *see* Mental retardation
Rh disease:
  amniotic fluid examination, 115–117
  detection of Rh incompatibility, 113–114
  induction of labor and, 102, 114
  infertility and, 171
  pregnancy and, 111–119
  prevention of, 118–119
Rh factors, *see* Rh disease
Rh immunoglobulin, 118–119
  See also Rh disease
Rh incompatibility, *see* Rh disease
"Rh negative," 111
  See also Rh disease
"Rh positive," 111
  See also Rh disease
Rhesus monkey, 111, 153
Rheumatic fever, *see* Heart disease
Rhinoplasty ("nose job"), 208–209
Rhythm method, 37, 38
  See also Contraceptives
Rhytidectomy (face-lift), 209
Rock, Dr. John, 15, 17, 37
Roman Catholic Church, *see* Catholic Church
Rome, ancient, 4, 5, 56, 197
Rubber, *see* Condom
Rubella (German measles):
  abortion and, 60, 80
  birth defects and, 140–141
  syndrome, 141
  vaccine, 141–142
Rubin test, for tubal patency, 43, 188

INDEX

Rupture of the membranes, 102, 107

Safe period, 7, 37
  See also Contraceptives
Salpingectomy, 42
Salpinx, 42
Sanger, Mrs. Margaret, 8
Scrotum, 44, 174
  fetal, 116
  sac, scrotal, 174
  temperature, intrascrotal, 176, 177–178
  varicocele, 168, 177
"Second-thoughts pill," 52
  See also Birth control
Section, caesarean, see Caesarean section
Semen, 45, 168, 170
  artificial insemination, 166, 191–193
  collection for sperm counts, 175
  ducts, seminal, 44, 168, 174
  examination of, 174–176
  frozen human, 192–193
  infertility and, 173, 175–177
  male sterilization and, 44–45
  penetration test, 186
  vesicles, seminal, 44, 174
  withdrawal and, 32–33
  See also Sperm
Sequential contraceptive pill, 17
  See also Contraceptives
de Sévigné, Madame, 5
Sex conversion operations, 212–213
Sex education, need for, 48–49
Sex-exchange surgery, 212–213
"Sex transformation" surgery, 212–213
Sexual intercourse, see Sexual relations
Sexual relations:
  abstinence, 105–107, 170, 187
  ejaculation and, 33
  without ejaculation, 7
  felonious, and abortion, 75–77
  infertility and, 167, 170–171, 173, 175, 177, 183
  in the later years, 215–218
  during menstruation, 31
  during and after pregnancy, 106–107
  in rhythm method, 37–38
  after "sex transformation" surgery, 213
Sexual response, postmenopausal, 216–217
SIECUS (Sex Information and Education Council of the U.S.), 13
Silicones, 208, 211
Simple mastectomy, 204
Sims-Huhner test (postcoital), 186
Skin:
  acne scars, treatment of, 210
  elasticity of, 199, 209
  graft, for frown wrinkles, 209–210
  graft, in infertility research, 171
Skin condom, 5, 30–31
  See also Contraceptives
Society for the Suppression of Vice, 7
Spallanzani, Lazzaro, 192
Spanish fly, 217
Sparteine, 102
Sperm:
  collection for sperm counts, 174–176
  ducts, 168, 174
  heads, abnormal, 176–177
  infertility and, 168, 173, 175–177
  motility of, 33, 174–175
  spermatogenesis, 16, 168, 173–174, 176, 177, 178
  after vasectomy, 44
  See also Semen
Spinnbarkeit, 186
Sponges, contraceptive, 6, 38–39
  See also Contraceptives
Spontaneous abortion, see Abortion

INDEX

Sterility, 165, 167
  abortion and, 81–82
  radiation and, 44, 168
Sterility and fertility, 165–193
  See also Male infertility *and* Female infertility
Sterilization, 41–45
  compulsory, 45
  female, nonsurgical procedures, 43–44
  female, surgical procedures, 42–43
  indications for, 41–42
  legal aspects of, 45
  male, surgical procedures, 44–45
  reversal of female, 43
  reversal of male, 45
  voluntary, 41–45
Stoics, 56
Stone, Dr. Hannah, 8
Suppositories, vaginal, 4, 36
  See also Contraceptives
Stillbirth, 95, 121, 122, 141
Syphilis, *see* Venereal disease

Tablets, vaginal, *see* Foam
di Tagliacozzi, Dr. Gasparo, 207
"Taking care," *see* Withdrawal
Tampons, contraceptive, 4, 6, 39
  See also Contraceptives
Temperature, basal body:
  automatic recording of, 183–184
  ovulation determination, 182, 183–184, 190
  rhythm method and, 37–38
Testes (testicles), 16, 44, 168, 173–174
  plastic, 213
Testosterone, 174, 177
Tests for pregnancy, 87–90
Teutons, ancient, 3
Thalidomide, 139–140
Thermography, 202–203

Thrombophlebitis:
  abortion, self-induced, and, 82
  The Pill and, 21
Thyroid gland, 149, 170, 177, 184, 209
Tietze, Dr. Christopher, 83
Toxemia of pregnancy, 91, 92, 102, 149, 150, 158
Transfusion, blood, 121
  exchange, in Rh disease, 114
  hemophiliac bleeding and, 126
  hemorrhage in pregnancy and, 91
  intrauterine, in Rh disease, 117
  placental, 149
Transsexualism, 212–213
Transvestism, 212
Tubal insufflation, 43, 188
Tubal ligation, 42
Tubal patency, 43, 188, 189
Tubal surgery, 189–190
Tuberculosis:
  abortion and, 60, 70, 95–96
  pregnancy and, 95–96
Tubes, *see* Fallopian tubes
Tumors, fibroid, 170, 190, 191

Ultrasonic holographic beams, 203
Ultrasound waves, in obstetrics, 93
Umbilical cord, 113, 114, 149, 158
U.S. Food and Drug Administration, 15, 185
Urethra:
  penile, 34, 174
  prostatic, 44
Urinary pregnanediol test, 183
Urinary tract infections, during pregnancy, 96–97
Uterus:
  cancer of, 21, 58, 204–205
  cornua of, 6, 42, 43
  curettage of, 80
  "D and C," 80

Uterus (*continued*)
  double, 170, 190, 191
  endometrial biopsy, 182, 190
  endometrium, 181
  fibroid tumors of, 170, 190, 191
  hysterectomy, 43, 58
  hysterotomy, 80
  hysterosalpingography, 188–189
  infertility and, 169, 170, 190–191
  intrauterine life, 115–117
  intrauterine transfusion, 117
  muscle of, 181, 191
  removal of (hysterectomy), 43, 58
  rupture of, from self-induced abortion, 82
  "unicorn," 170

Vagina:
  absence of, 213
  artificial, 213
  douches for, 6, 28, 36, 38, 39, 40
    See also Contraceptives
  infections of, 31, 199
  infertility and, 170, 187
  smears of, 183, 185, 199
Vaginal sponge, 6, 38–39
  See also Contraceptives
Vaginismus, 187
Vaginitis, 31, 213
Varicocele, 168, 177
Vas deferens, 44, 45

Vasectomy (vas resection), 44–45
Venereal disease:
  gonorrhea, 48, 168
  in minors, 47–48
  prevention of, 5, 31
  syphilis, 48, 169
Virility and infertility, 173
Voluntary sterilization, *see* Sterilization

Wallerstein, Dr. H., 114
Wiener, Dr. Alexander, 111
"Wild Boy of Aveyron," 155–156
Wilson's disease, 127, 160
Withdrawal, 6, 7, 32–34
  "being careful," 32
  coitus incompletus, 32
  coitus interruptus, 6, 32, 34
  coitus reservatus, 7, 32
  coitus saxonicus, 32
  Karezza, 7, 32
  onanism, 32
  risks of, 32–33
  sperm counts and, 175
  "taking care," 32
Womb, *see* Uterus

Xerography, 203
X-ray:
  abortion and, 81
  breast cancer treatment, 203–204
  sterilization and, 44

RG
136
B38
1969

JUL 19 1973